The Wealth Question

What God Thinks About Prosperity

Donvan Ochieng' Odhiambo

Contents

Title Page
Copyright
Introduction
1. Right Mindset 1
2. Is Money your god? 9
3. Is Money Important? 14
4. Heavenly Riches vs. Earthly Riches 17
5. Holiness before Wealth and Giving 23
6. The prosperity of God's Covenant People 27
7. Heritage of the Righteous 38
8. Poverty 41
9. The Love of God 50
10. Living Testimonies 53
11. Christian and Lacking 57
12. Wealth for the Kingdom 68
13. Clash of Kingdoms 73
14. Seven Keys to Accumulating Wealth 85
15. God's Supernatural Provision 100

16. Traps of Wealth 109
17. Generosity 118
18. The Conclusion 122
Acknowledgments 125
About The Author 127
Books By This Author 129

Introduction

Growing up in Kenya, I desperately wanted a bicycle so that I could bike around like other kids in my neighborhood. With much excitement, I made an offer to my parents that if I became the top of my class, they would buy me one. They agreed.

I worked hard and became the first in my class numerous times. However, my father could not meet his end of the bargain each time I handed him my report card. I knew he sincerely wanted to get me a bike, but he just couldn't afford it. He would urge me to keep on working hard, hoping that one day he would be in a position to buy me one.

I continued to excel in school, although I ended up growing up without ever owning a bike. I learned the value of education and continued to work hard even without having the bike to motivate me.

When I realized that financing my high school education would be difficult for my family, I decided to work even harder to make sure I got a scholarship spot at one of Kenya's top high schools called Starehe Boys' Center.

I made a covenant with God asking Him to open doors for me to get into the school when I was in grade eight. The Lord did, and I joined Starehe.

Later, God again opened doors for me to join Amherst College, an elite school in Massachusetts. This time too, I was on a full scholarship and therefore didn't have to pay a dime for my college education.

Over the years, I realized that God used my background to develop in me a strong empathy for the poor and a desire to know the truth of His word concerning finances. I went through a period of in-depth study and seeking God concerning the same. In this book, I will share what I have been learning over the years.

1. Right Mindset

Is money evil? There is a massive debate going on right now in Christian circles concerning God's view on material prosperity.

On one side, everyone questions the intention of any preacher who talks about wealth. Some consider this topic misguided at best, or even demonic at worst. Others go to the extent of equating talking about finances to being worldly, non-spiritual, or earthly-focused.

On the other side is the view that those who are against any preaching about material prosperity are unrealistic and advocating for poverty.

Who is right? What should we believe? In this case, as in all things, the word of God should be our guide.

We have to think about the definition of money and determine the right attitude to have towards it. The apostle Paul took this approach when he, under the inspiration of the Spirit, addressed the issue in 1 Timothy 6, which is one of the most quoted scriptures on this subject.

We will analyze the passage in its entirety so that we don't make the mistake of quoting scriptures out of context. Unfortunately, as we will see, this scripture is often quoted partially – most people quote the first part without going through the rest of the chapter.

1 Timothy 6:6-10, 17-19 reads:

> [6] Now godliness with contentment is great gain. [7] For
> we brought nothing into *this* world, *and it is* certain
> we can carry nothing out. [8] And having food and
> clothing, with these we shall be content. [9] But those
> who desire to be rich fall into temptation and a
> snare, and *into* many foolish and harmful lusts which
> drown men in destruction and perdition. [10] For the
> love of money is a root of all *kinds of* evil, for which
> some have strayed from the faith in their greediness,
> and pierced themselves through with many sorrows...
> [17] Command those who are rich in this present age
> not to be haughty, nor to trust in uncertain riches but
> in the living God, who gives us richly all things to
> enjoy. [18] *Let them* do good, that they be rich in good
> works, ready to give, willing to share, [19] storing up for
> themselves a good foundation for the time to come,
> that they may lay hold on eternal life.

First Part (1 Timothy 6:6-10)

- *"[6] Now godliness with contentment is great gain."*

The passage starts in verse 6 by urging us to live godly lives and to be content with whatever we have.

Said differently, we should be thankful and at peace, whether we have abundant material possessions or not. So then, this verse is saying that being content in whatever situation is the right attitude to have towards material wealth.

As a point of note, the Holy Spirit, through Paul, taught the same thing in the epistle to the Philippians.

Philippians 4:11-12 says, "[11] ... I have learned in whatever state I am, to be content: [12] I know how to be abased, and I know how to abound. Everywhere and in all things I have learned both to be full and to be hungry, both to abound and to suffer need."

- *"[7] For we brought nothing into this world, and it is certain we can carry nothing out. [8] And having food and clothing, with these we shall be content."*

In verses 7 and 8, Paul emphasized the reality that we didn't bring any material possessions with us when we were born. Similarly, we will not carry anything with us when we depart from the earth.

In other words, the Bible is pointing out that having a proper understanding of eternity should help us prioritize things correctly. Keeping in mind that our lives on earth will come to an end should help us live wisely.

Thus, God, speaking through Paul, was instructing us to have the right priorities and values in life.

- *"[9] But those who desire to be rich fall into temptation and a snare, and into many foolish and harmful lusts which drown men in destruction and perdition."*

First, verse 9 begins with a 'but', which indicates that we should view what comes next in contrast to what Paul wrote right before.

This verse warns that those who seek wealth are falling into a trap. Paul called such pursuits foolish and harmful.

Realize that the definition of a fool is someone who doesn't think ahead. A fool is a person whose immediate actions are not guided by the consequences of his decisions.

Considering what the apostle wrote in verses 7 and 8, verse 9 is therefore **warning against pursuing wealth without reckoning eternity**.

Said differently, verse 9 is saying that **it is foolish to continuously seek wealth if we don't keep in mind that our lives on earth will one day come to an end**.

- *"10 For the love of money is a root of all kinds of evil, for which some have strayed from the faith in their greediness, and pierced themselves through with many sorrows."*

In verse 10, the apostle plainly points out that we should not have the 'love of money'.

To better understand what the word of God means by the 'love of money', we need to have a clear picture of the meaning of love:

To love something, according to the Biblical standard, is to be willing to lay down our lives for that thing – Song of Solomon 8:6 declares that love is as strong as death. Moreover, Jesus Christ, in proving His love for humanity, laid down His life for us (John 15:13).

It follows, therefore, that when we love money, we are willing to sacrifice everything for the sake of it. To obtain more, we would do anything that goes against loving God and loving others, which is the Biblical definition of sin. That means we are willing to die spiritually.

Such an attitude is what the Bible calls 'loving money', greed, or covetousness (1 Timothy 6:10).

Notice that the willingness to sin to get money is precisely why the 'love of money' is called a form of idolatry. This is because an idol is something we serve like a god and so are willing to lay down our lives for it.

Actually, Colossians 3:5 (emphasis added) clearly defines the love of money as such. The passage says, "Therefore put to death your members which are on the earth: fornication, uncleanness, passion, evil desire, and **covetousness, which is idolatry**."

The book of Job is another example that shows that 'loving money' is a form of idolatry. In Job 31, Job mentions putting trust in money in the same breath as the idolatry of worshipping the sun and moon.

Job 31:24-28 (ESV) reads,

> 24 If I have made gold my trust
> or called fine gold my confidence,
> 25 if I have rejoiced because my wealth was abundant
> or because my hand had found much,
> 26 if I have looked at the sun when it shone,
> or the moon moving in splendor,
> 27 and my heart has been secretly enticed,
> and my mouth has kissed my hand,
> 28 this also would be an iniquity to be punished by the judges,
> for I would have been false to God above.

Summary

So far, we have established that Paul points out three mindsets God wants us to have concerning material wealth:

1. We should always be content.
2. We should not forget that earthly things are temporary.
3. We should not love money.

Second Part (1 Timothy 6:17-19)
Now, let's go to the second part of this scripture, which is less talked about even though it is equally crucial if we are to have a complete view of what the Bible is saying:

- *"[17] Command those who are rich in this present age not to be haughty, nor to trust in uncertain riches but in the living God, who gives us richly all things to enjoy. [18] Let them do good, that they be rich in good works, ready to give, willing to share, [19] storing up for themselves a good foundation for the time to come, that they may lay hold on eternal life."*

In verses 17-19, Paul directly addressed those who are rich in material possessions. The apostle emphasized that the rich should be careful not to let pride grow in their hearts when he wrote that the wealthy should remain humble.

Recognize that with humility comes the acknowledgment that our lives depend on God (Deuteronomy 8:10-17). Consequently, humility always leads to honoring the Lord because of the understanding that everything we have is from Him.

Paul's warning is especially relevant to the rich: A wealthy person is more susceptible to be lifted in pride since they can more readily meet their needs. As a result, they may not see the need for God.

We see this around us all the time. How many times have we read or heard of someone boasting that they don't need God because they can solve all their problems? Or that God is only for poor people looking for an escape?

That said, when a wealthy person maintains their relationship with God and continues to trust in Him, that individual is demonstrating humility. Moreover, it is worth noting that the very fact that the Bible instructs the rich to be humble means that it is possible to be wealthy and still maintain humility towards the Lord.

Summary

We can draw three important conclusions from this section (1 Timothy 6:17-19):

• First, this passage is pointing out that, ultimately, God is the source of wealth when it says that He abundantly provides all things for us to enjoy (v 17). This statement is true because we can trace back all wealth to God's creation — whether minerals, plants, land, or the abilities of man.

The understanding that God is the source of wealth leads to the conclusion that riches are not inherently evil. The simple reason is that the Lord God can't be the source of something wicked.

• Secondly, in verse 18, the word of God instructs us to use riches as a means to do good to those around us.

This statement also proves that wealth is not inherently sinful. We can use wealth for good, or we can use it for evil. It is upon us to decide. Something is not automatically bad just because someone has used it in the wrong way.

• And, lastly, using riches to do good to others is one way of accumulating treasures for eternal life (v19).

Based on the above, we can accurately conclude that nowhere does this passage indicate that being wealthy is displeasing to God. Instead, covetousness is what the Bible condemns.

Made Wealthy by God

Throughout the Bible, God never condemns wealth as sinful. Observe that the word of God clearly defines sin and then instructs us to get rid of it. However, that is never the case with wealth. Instead, the Bible directs us to use wealth in the right way.

In fact, Proverbs 10:22 states that God's blessing produces riches without causing any sorrow. Furthermore, there are instances in the Bible where God made people wealthy. Job and Abraham are good examples:

- Job 43:12-17 states that Job owned thousands of sheep, camels, oxen and donkeys. God blessed him with great wealth in addition to a big and beautiful family.

- Genesis 13:2 says that Abraham had a lot of livestock, silver and gold, as a result of God's blessings.

To conclude, this may be surprising to some, but the word of God tells us to enjoy the blessings that the Lord has given us. For example, Ecclesiastes 5:19 declares that having wealth and being able to enjoy it is a gift from God. Therefore, we are to be grateful for the ability to enjoy what we own.

2. Is Money your god?

Balaam's Case

One of the most tragic stories in the Old Testament is that of Balaam (Numbers 22-24). Balaam was a true prophet of God when he started ministry. He clearly understood the ways of the Lord, as demonstrated by his ability to call on God and receive responses from heaven (Numbers 22). As a matter of fact, God granted him the grace to see visions, including the Lord Himself (Numbers 22:9, 31).

Despite all this, the love of money was a hidden evil in the prophet's heart. This weakness manifested when Balak, the king of Moab, sent emissaries to ask Balaam to help him oppose Israel (Numbers 22).

People in those days understood that spirit beings existed. Consequently, it was common practice for kings to speak a curse in the name of their gods to defeat their enemies in battle (Numbers 22:6, 1 Samuel 17:43).

For that reason, Balak sought Balaam to curse the Israelites in the name of God. In return, Balak would give Balaam silver and gold.

At first, Balaam refused to go to the king of Moab. Even so, it seems that the prophet's heart was inclined to receiving the promised riches in reward for cursing Israel. The evidence of this is that, at the request of Balak, Balaam continued to ask the Lord to permit him to go even after God had said that He wanted to bless and not curse Israel. The Lord eventually allowed Balaam to go to Balak but then made it very clear that He was displeased with the prophet.

I always wondered why God was so stern with Balaam despite giving him the green light to go until I understood that the Lord corrects those He loves. In my view, God wanted to correct Balaam's heart and also change the situation in favor of Israel so that the prophet would bless and not curse them.

When Balaam was on his way to Balak, the Lord delivered a spectacular warning to him: God enabled the prophet's donkey to speak and also opened Balaam's eyes to see the Angel of the Lord standing with a sword in hand, ready to strike.

The Angel's message was plain: Balaam's ways were perverted. The Lord could have killed him, but He chose not to. The fact that God refrained means that He did not want to destroy Balaam. The Lord wanted him to repent. Lovingly, God revealed Balaam's error so that he could correct it.

For a moment, Balaam corrected himself and prophesied precisely what God said. He gave a series of prophecies, including one about the coming of the Lord Jesus Christ.

Balaam's story, however, ended tragically because he later advised the Moabite king to entice Israel into idolatry and sexual immorality (Numbers 31:16, Revelation 2:14). These two sins would then lead to the destruction of Israel.

Jude 1:11 reveals that Balaam's motivation for giving that advice was money. He chose not to obey God when he advised the Moabites on how to orchestrate the destruction of Israel. The prophet was willing to see people destroyed and lives lost so that he could gain money. Sadly, one who used to be a prophet of God ended up becoming a false prophet and died when Israel conquered Canaan (Joshua 13:22).

Thus, in Balaam, we find an example of someone who once walked intimately with God but loved money more than he loved God and people.

Judas' Case

Judas had a unique opportunity in that he was one of the first 12 apostles of the Lord. He was privileged to receive all of Jesus' teachings firsthand and in more detail – the Lord would go to greater lengths to explain things to the twelve that were harder for the multitudes to understand (Mark 4:33-34, Matt 13:34-36).

The apostle saw all the miracles that Jesus performed. He was there when the Lord supernaturally drove out demons, healed the sick, raised the dead, multiplied food, and fed thousands (Luke 9:10-16). Judas himself even performed some miraculous signs in Jesus' name (Luke 9:1-6).

No doubt, the apostle had a depth of fellowship with God that most of us have not attained. Recall that he spent most of his days and nights with the Lord for the three years that Jesus Christ executed His earthly ministry.

Judas, like Balaam, had a love for money that became evident when he began stealing money from the treasury of the Lord and the apostles (John 12:1-7). His passion for money grew to the extent that he was willing to betray Jesus when the opportunity presented itself (Matt 26:14-16).

The Last Supper was Judas' opportunity to repent. Amazingly, during that eventful night, the Lord pointed out to him that He was aware of the evil that Judas was planning in his heart (Matt 26:25).

The apostle knew that what the Lord said was true. Sadly, however, Judas had made up his mind and nothing was going to change it.

After the warning from Jesus at the Last Supper, Satan entered Judas and took over completely. What followed was a chain of events that ended in the apostle hanging himself because of the guilt of betraying the Lord (John 13, Matthew 27). Just like Jesus had said, it would have been better for Judas if he had not been born (Matthew 26:24). He died in his sin and ended up condemned to eternal judgment because money had become his god.

The Evidence of our Devotion

In life, we will always have to decide what is more important to us. Whatever we choose is what we love. Whether we love God or money becomes apparent when a situation arises where seeking monetary gain and doing the will of God are at odds.

Jesus warned us about facing this dilemma in Matthew 6:24. He said that no one can serve two masters. It is impossible to be faithful to both. Either God is our Lord or money is. We have to decide what to hate and what to love. We have to choose to whom we will be devoted.

In Matthew 6, Lord Jesus Christ gave us the right priorities to have. The essence of what the Lord said was that we are to have faith in God (Matthew 6:25); we are to desire more than anything to be part of His kingdom and do His work, and we are to have His righteousness evident in our lives. Then, God will add to us every material possession that we need (Matthew 6:33).

3. Is Money Important?

A close friend of mine once called me wondering what I thought about a prophetic word he had just received. The message was about God prospering him. He was honestly concerned about whether it was from God or not and sought clarification about the importance of money in the life of a believer in Christ. The internal conflict came about because the word seemed contrary to what my friend thought the Bible said.

In my experience, this question comes up a lot. I have encountered some who know they have a calling into the finance industry, or have the grace to make money but feel guilty about employing their talents. They were taught implicitly or explicitly that making money is not essential for a Christian.

Does the Bible ever acknowledge that it is vital to have financial resources? If yes, what are the limits to the importance of money?

This question is better understood when we take time to consider what the Lord prayed in the Gospel of John.

In John 17:14-15, Jesus asked the Father, "[14] I have given them Your word; and the world has hated them because they are not of the world, just as I am not of the world. [15] I do not pray that You should take them out of the world, but that You should keep them from the evil one."

Not being of the world means that our values or mindsets should not be like those who do not know God. Primarily, the attitude of the world is to embrace sin while, as Christians, we should not. That is why the Bible says friendship with the world is enmity with God (James 4:4).

The consequence of the church being in the world is that we will have to operate within the systems of the world. That is, there are things that we will do, just like any other person would.

For example, we are still citizens of our respective countries, and thus, we participate in the affairs of our nation just like any other citizen would. We still have to pay taxes wherever we live because we make use of resources and benefit from the services of the government.

It is worth pointing out that the Lord Himself exemplified this principle when He paid taxes in Matthew 17:24-27. In fact, He performed a miracle to pay the temple tax when He told Peter to get money from the fish's mouth.

The Financial System

The world works by exchanging goods and services for money. Consequently, we will need money to fulfill the goals and visions God has given us. The question of how much money depends on the things we have to accomplish.

Thus, to say that we don't need material wealth or money to conduct the affairs of God (and our own) in the world would be dishonest.

Actually, the wisdom books of the Bible, Proverbs and Ecclesiastes, have a lot to say about the importance of finances:

In Proverbs 10:15, wealth is likened to a fortress to the rich and poverty described as damaging to the poor. This analogy of wealth as a fortress denotes that having financial means is a strong position to be in. Unquestionably, when we have financial resources, we can more easily carry out our mission in life, which can be summed up in one word, love.

Furthermore, in Ecclesiastes 7:11-12, wisdom and money are both described as a defense. Therefore, we can infer that both are important. However, wisdom is more important because it can save one's life.

Lastly, the Bible does not refute that wealth brings joy in the natural. It depicts money as the solution to some problems. Ecclesiastes 10:19 (ESV, emphasis added) notes,

> 19 Bread is made for laughter,
> and wine gladdens life,
> and **money answers everything**.

4. Heavenly Riches vs. Earthly Riches

The Bible describes Job as one of the wealthiest people of his time. This man of God was successful by every measure.

The scripture records that he "... was blameless and upright, and one who feared God and shunned evil. [2] And seven sons and three daughters were born to him. [3] Also, his possessions were seven thousand sheep, three thousand camels, five hundred yoke of oxen, five hundred female donkeys, and a very large household, so that this man was the greatest of all the people of the East." (Job 1:1-3)

Despite this, during the toughest time of his life, Job proclaimed, "[21] ... Naked I came from my mother's womb, and naked shall I return. The Lord gave, and the Lord has taken away; blessed be the name of the Lord." (Job 1:21, ESV)

Later, King Solomon, one of the wealthiest and wisest people ever to live, came to the same conclusion in the book of Ecclesiastes:

Ecclesiastes 5:15-17 notes that every person was born with nothing. Similarly, when a person dies, they take nothing with them to the afterlife. There's not one thing that man has accumulated through their hard work that will go beyond the grave.

These two very wealthy men, Job and Solomon, were pointing out a vital truth that God wants us to reckon. We should always remember that we will not take our earthly riches with us to eternity. They will not be useful to us when our life on earth ends because we can't carry them with us beyond our existence here.

The Lord impressed the same message in the parable of the rich fool in Luke 12:13-21:

In that parable, the rich man was enjoying his wealth and planning to expand his storage rooms when, suddenly, God told him that he was a fool and that he was going to die that night.

The man seemed to have forgotten that he would leave behind everything for which he had worked. He was a fool because he didn't care to use his earthly riches to lay up treasures in heaven and so be rich toward God. This, therefore, means that the rich man was not thinking about wealth in the right way.

Jesus Christ wanted all His disciples to know that the measure of success in life is not how much money we have accumulated. Instead, the correct gauge is the heavenly riches we have.

To reiterate, the Bible is emphatic that God values heavenly riches more than earthly riches. There's no comparison between the two in His eyes.

For example, in the book of Revelation, Jesus described the church at Smyrna as wealthy, even though they lacked in terms of earthly riches (Revelation 2:9-11). On the contrary, He referred to the Laodicean church, which was wealthy in worldly terms, as wretched, miserable, poor, blind, and naked because they were lukewarm. The Laodiceans were not zealous for the Lord (Revelation

3:14-19).

Earthly Riches are a Test

Earthly riches are a test for us in the sense that they reveal what is truly important to us. The way we use our resources indicates what is in our hearts or the things that we hold dear.

The Lord demonstrated the concept that material riches are a test when He told the rich young ruler to sell all he had and give the proceeds to the poor (Mark 10:17-27).

Through that instruction, Jesus intended to reveal what lay hidden in the young man's heart. Contrary to what the rich young ruler thought of himself, his reluctance to obey proved that he loved his wealth more than he loved God.

Although not everyone undergoes the same test of being asked to give everything away, what we do with whatever we have still reveals the inclinations of our hearts.

Our decisions concerning money reveal the good or bad in our hearts that we may not even be aware of. What we can be sure of is that when we devote our resources to demonstrating love to the Lord and humanity, then we are people genuinely after God's heart.

Earthly Riches are Tools

Any wise investor will tell you that they are looking for investments that will bear fruit. Anything else is not worth the time or effort.

Similarly, our focus should be building things that will bear fruit for eternity, something that will last. **The consequence of understanding this is that material riches will be valuable to us only as far as we use them to gain**

heavenly riches.

Therefore, we should view earthly riches as instruments of obtaining something greater, eternal riches. That is to say that **material things should not be the end goal but tools for a higher purpose**.

Furthermore, the Bible teaches us that the thought of taking nothing with us at the end of our journey on earth should sober us enough to use our wealth for eternal purposes and so become rich in God's eyes.

Jesus summarized this truth in two parts in Luke 16:1-13:

1. Recognize that there is an eternity.
In the parable of the Unjust Steward, the Lord emphasized that the wisdom of the steward was that he used his present influence to position himself for a better future.

In Luke 16:9-12, the Lord said that we should use our currencies on the earth to build our lives after this world. He likened using our money for enduring purposes to making friendships with those who will later give us help when we need it.

Jesus also pointed out that when we are faithful in little things, we will be faithful in more important things. Similarly, when we are unfaithful in small things, we will be unfaithful in more significant things. If we can be devoted to God with earthly currency, then the Lord can entrust us with eternal riches.

2. Our commitment should always be to God and not money.
Luke 16:13 states that "13 No servant can serve two masters; for either he will hate the one and love the other, or else he

will be loyal to the one and despise the other. You cannot serve God and mammon."

How to Build Heavenly Riches

The Bible teaches that one of the ways to build heavenly riches is by demonstrating love using our earthly riches.

Generosity is a foundational principle that everyone who believes in Jesus Christ should practice. This is because giving is a demonstration of the love of God in our hearts. And, when we are full of love, it will be natural for us to want to use whatever we have to help the needy.

On numerous occasions, the Bible encourages us to make use of our earthly riches to demonstrate love to those around us. For example, Ephesians 4:28 says that those who used to steal should not steal any more. Instead, they should learn to work hard and earn an honest living so that they could be in a financial position to be charitable.

In response to our deeds of generosity, the Lord notes our actions and then rewards us by allocating heavenly treasures to each of us. Those treasures will remain with us for eternity:

In Luke 12:32-34 (ESV), Jesus said, "[32] "Fear not, little flock, for it is your Father's good pleasure to give you the kingdom. [33] Sell your possessions, and give to the needy. Provide yourselves with moneybags that do not grow old, with a treasure in the heavens that does not fail, where no thief approaches and no moth destroys. [34] For where your treasure is, there will your heart be also."

Additionally, Matthew 19:21 records Jesus' advice to the rich young ruler that if he wanted perfection, he should sell everything, give alms to the poor and then follow Him.

In so doing, he would have treasures stored up for him in heaven.

Other scriptures that support the concept that God will reward every charitable deed when we get to heaven include Matthew 6:3-4, 1 Timothy 6:17-19, and 2 Timothy 1:16-18.

The implication of all this is that our position before God in eternity will be determined by how much we learned to demonstrate our love toward Him and humanity in various ways, including through our generosity (Luke 16:11).

5. Holiness before Wealth and Giving

[11] When I was a child, I spoke as a child, I understood as a child, I thought as a child; ***but when I became a man, I put away childish things****.*

– 1 Corinthians 13:11 (emphasis added)

The book of Corinthians teaches us to become mature in our thinking by having the right priorities. In God's view, being motivated by love is the most important thing (1 Corinthians 13:13).

For clarity, walking in holiness is walking in love, and walking in love is walking in holiness. The two are equivalent according to Scripture.

To elaborate, walking in holiness means to walk according to the commandments of God. And, in the New Testament, the Lord summarized all commandments into one, love—love for God and love for all humanity (Matthew 22:37-40). Therefore, we are, in essence, talking about walking in love when we talk about holiness.

In Matthew 6:33, Jesus Christ instructed us to seek first His kingdom and His righteousness, and He would add all other things to us. This scripture means that we should prioritize holiness or love over finances and material things.

Love is the Greatest

Throughout Scripture, God emphasizes that walking with Him in love is more important than having an abundance of material things:

• In Song of Songs, King Solomon pointed out that love is greater than wealth.

Song of Songs 8:7 (ESV) says,

> 7 Many waters cannot quench love,
> neither can floods drown it.
> If a man offered for love
> all the wealth of his house,
> he would be utterly despised.

• As one would expect, the book of Proverbs touches on this theme many times. Proverbs 28:6 declares that it is better to be poor and blameless than to be rich and perverse. Again, in Proverbs 15:16, the word of God says that it is better to have a little with the fear of the Lord than to have great treasure without honoring God.

• According to Jeremiah 9:23-24 (ESV, emphasis added),

> 23 Thus says the Lord: "Let not the wise man boast in his wisdom, let not the mighty man boast in his might, **let not the rich man boast in his riches, 24 but let him who boasts boast in this, that he understands and knows me, that I am the Lord who practices steadfast love, justice, and righteousness in the earth**. For in these things I delight, declares the Lord.

• Haggai tells us that when we are living in rebellion against God's word, our offerings are not acceptable before Him. That means that God prioritizes righteousness over any offerings we could ever give.

Haggai 2:14 states (ESV), "[14] ... "So is it with this people, and with this nation before me, declares the Lord, and so with every work of their hands. And what they offer there is unclean."

God is everything

We have everything when we have God because He is the Source of all things, including wealth. The word of God expressly promises that He will add prosperity to those who prioritize seeking Him and His righteousness (Matthew 6:33).

As an illustration, the Psalmist went through life unshaken because he understood that he had everything he needed as long as God was with him.

In Psalm 23, David wrote that the Lord was his shepherd and so he would not lack anything. God would provide everything he needed the same way a shepherd provides for his sheep by taking them to areas with green pastures and still waters. Furthermore, the Lord would always guide and help him live a holy life because of His love.

The Psalmist confessed that he would not fear even if he walked through the valley of the shadow of death (where death rules). Even in such a place, nothing could move him because the Lord would always be with him. He asserted that God's rod (His power) and staff (His guidance) would be a source of great comfort. The Lord would prepare a feast for the Psalmist despite the presence of adversaries.

David noted that the Lord is generous with His grace. Therefore, the goodness and mercy of God would follow him all the days of his life. And, he would dwell in the house of the Lord forever!

In addition to the Psalmist, the Bible records many kings of Israel and Judah who experienced prosperity because they focused on loving God and obeying His commands. Abundance came after they prioritized the ways of God. Jehoshaphat and Hezekiah are examples of these:

- Concerning Jehoshaphat, 2 Chronicles 17:5-6 says:

> 5 Therefore the Lord established the kingdom in his hand; and all Judah gave presents to Jehoshaphat, and he had riches and honor in abundance. 6 And his heart took delight in the ways of the Lord; moreover he removed the high places and wooden images from Judah.

- About Hezekiah, the word of God notes:

> 5 He trusted in the Lord God of Israel, so that after him was none like him among all the kings of Judah, nor who were before him. 6 For he held fast to the Lord; he did not depart from following Him, but kept His commandments, which the Lord had commanded Moses. 7 The Lord was with him; he prospered wherever he went. And he rebelled against the king of Assyria and did not serve him. (2 Kings 18:5-7)

6. The prosperity of God's Covenant People

In exploring the subject of wealth, it is crucial to look at God's dealings with humanity right from the beginning through the lens of this topic. The reason for this approach is that, according to the Scriptures, God never changes (Numbers 23:19, Hebrews 13:8, James 1:17). His likes and dislikes do not change with time.

In light of that truth, we should observe God's attitude towards wealth in the beginning and then notice the consistency of that attitude throughout the Bible. When we study the lives of those who have been in a covenant relationship with God right from Adam and Eve to the patriarchs, Israel, and the church, we should see a consistent pattern of God's will concerning the prosperity of His covenant people.

a. Adam and Eve

The book of Genesis reveals how God created man, both male and female, in His image and likeness. He gave them dominion over all of His creation on the earth (Genesis 1:26-28). God, who clearly delighted in Adam and Eve, blessed the first man and woman and placed them in the Garden of Eden.

When we read the detailed description of the Garden of Eden in Genesis 2:8-15, it becomes apparent that it was a lovely place with abundant natural resources. The dwelling place of Adam and Eve before the fall had plenty of water, every kind of pleasant tree, fruits, gold, precious stones, and minerals.

Since God originally intended that Adam and Eve, together with their descendants, have access to the Garden forever, we can conclude that it is God's perfect will for us to have an abundance of everything we need while we walk with Him and labor to fulfill His divine plan.

b. The Patriarchs

Abraham

The earth went through a process of decline after God drove Adam and Eve out of the Garden for their sin. The decay continued until the time of Noah when the Lord had to purge the world through the judgment of the flood (Genesis 6 and 7).

Even so, God continued the process of restoring His relationship with mankind after the fall. His plan of redemption continued to unfold after the flood with Noah's offspring and into the next age (the age of the patriarchs), which began with Abraham.

The Lord spelled out His intentions for Abraham's life right from when He called him: God would give Abraham so many descendants that he would not be able to count, make his name great, and bless him so that he would be a blessing to other people (Genesis 12:1-3).

The Lord blessed Abraham in all things (Genesis 24:1). And part of that blessing was an abundance of material possessions. This fact is demonstrated in Genesis 13:2, which spells out that Abraham was very rich in livestock, silver, and gold.

Abraham's story is essential because God refers to His dealings with him as a pattern of how He would deal with those who seek Him and keep His covenant.

For example, Isaiah 51:1-2 (ESV) says,

> 51 Listen to me, you who pursue righteousness,
> you who seek the Lord:
> look to the rock from which you were hewn,
> and to the quarry from which you were dug.
> 2 Look to Abraham your father
> and to Sarah who bore you;
> for he was but one when I called him,
> that I might bless him and multiply him.

Therefore, it is right to say that everyone who is in a covenant relationship with God should expect His blessings in every area, including finances.

Isaac and Jacob

The blessings of God continued in the lives of Isaac and Jacob, who were Abraham's son and grandson, respectively.

The Lord multiplied Isaac's material possessions. The book of Genesis tells a story of how God supernaturally increased his harvest.

Genesis 26:12-14 records that Isaac sowed during a time of drought and famine. He reaped a harvest that was a hundred times what he planted because of the blessing of the Lord upon him. God continued to prosper him so much that the Philistines, in whose territory he was dwelling, envied him.

Later, towards the end of his life, Isaac blessed his son

Jacob. His prayer shows that part of the blessing upon Jacob would be prosperity in material things:

Isaac asked the Lord to grant Jacob (later named Israel) the abundance of the earth. He prayed that his son would be the head in everything he undertook. Moreover, he specifically asked God to give Jacob 'of the dew of heaven', 'of the fatness of the earth', and an abundance of grain and wine (Genesis 27:28-29).

The Lord answered Isaac's prayer when Jacob became very prosperous during his time working for Laban (Genesis 30:40-43).

Later, Jacob acknowledged how God's supernatural hand was directly behind his prosperity (Genesis 32:9-10). In one instance, the Lord, through a dream, instructed him on how to acquire more sheep. He obeyed the instructions and ended up becoming very wealthy (see Genesis 31:10-13).

c. God's First Covenant Nation – Israel

The nation of Israel began their journey as God's first covenant nation when the Lord delivered them from bondage in Egypt.

The Lord didn't only deliver them from being slaves of Pharaoh and the Egyptians. They came out with an abundance of material possessions in fulfillment of the prophecy God gave Abraham about four hundred years earlier.

The Lord had told Abraham that his descendants would be strangers in a foreign land. They would be enslaved for four hundred years, after which God would bring them out with great possessions (Genesis 15:13-14).

In fulfillment of that promise, God gave the Israelites favor in the eyes of the Egyptians so that the Egyptians gave them whatever they asked for (Exodus 12:36). Thus, God was directly responsible for the riches Israel acquired.

Desert Years

God's provision for Israel's needs continued during their journey through the desert. In Deuteronomy 2:7, Moses pointed out to Israel that God had been concerned about their welfare. The Lord had been present with them and blessed whatever work they were involved in so that Israel could meet their needs.

Moreover, Moses reminded them that they were God's first covenant nation. He told them that the blessings of the Lord upon them as a people would continue as long as they continued walking in obedience to the Law that God had given them.

Deuteronomy 28:1-14 gives us a very detailed list of the areas in which the Lord promised to bless Israel if they remained righteous. Again, God's blessing upon the nation included an abundance of material riches.

Canaan

The Bible describes Canaan, the land that Israel inherited, as a very lush and fertile land.

In Deuteronomy 8:7-9, Moses described it as "[7]...good land, a land of brooks of water, of fountains and springs, that flow out of valleys and hills; [8] a land of wheat and barley, of vines and fig trees and pomegranates, a land of olive oil and honey; [9] a land in which you will eat bread without scarcity, in which you will lack nothing; a land whose stones *are* iron and out of whose hills you can dig copper."

Israel had inherited all of Canaan at the peak of their prosperity during King Solomon's era. The nation was so prosperous at that time that they considered silver to be of little value.

2 Chronicles 1:15 says, "[15] Also the king made silver and gold as common in Jerusalem as stones, and he made cedars as abundant as the sycamores which *are* in the lowland."

In summary, God fulfilled His desire to bless His covenant people by enabling Israel to conquer Canaan. The only condition that came with the prosperity was that they should not lose their love for the Lord. For their own sake, God warned the nation not to let the material possessions He had given them cause them to forget Him (Deuteronomy 6:10-12, Deuteronomy 11:13-17).

Restoration of Zion

Israel, however, fell many times. Even so, God, in His faithfulness, restored them each time. Unsurprisingly, the restoration of the nation after their downfall always included the restitution of their wealth.

For example, Isaiah 60 gives us a picture of Israel coming from captivity in ships laden with gold and silver, much like Israel came out of captivity from Egypt with a lot of wealth.

Isaiah 60:9 (ESV) reads,

[9] For the coastlands shall hope for me,
the ships of Tarshish first,
to bring your children from afar,

their silver and gold with them,
for the name of the Lord your God,
and for the Holy One of Israel,
because he has made you beautiful.

Jeremiah also prophesied about the restoration of Zion. He wrote that it would be full of rejoicing and abundance. And, there would be no more lack or sorrow (Jeremiah 31:12-14).

Similarly, Zechariah prophesied about God comforting Zion and filling her cities with abundant prosperity (Zechariah 1:17).

Therefore, taking everything into account, abundant blessings was God's will for Israel. Since Israel is an example of how the Lord deals with those in a covenant relationship with Him, we can say that God wants to bless everyone who honors Him.

d. The Church

The church refers to all of God's covenant people – both Jews and Gentiles. The Body of Christ includes everyone who has come into a covenant relationship with the Father through the shed blood of Jesus, the Messiah (Ephesians 2:11-22).

To understand God's will for the church concerning material riches, we'll turn to the epistles:

• When the apostle Paul addressed the issue of generosity in his letter to the Corinthian church, he noted that God could make all grace abound towards them so that they would have enough to help those in need.

2 Corinthians 9:5-8 (ESV) states,

> [5] So I thought it necessary to urge the brothers to go on ahead to you and arrange in advance for the gift you have promised, so that it may be ready as a willing gift, not as an exaction. [6] The point is this: whoever sows sparingly will also reap sparingly, and whoever sows bountifully will also reap bountifully. [7] Each one must give as he has decided in his heart, not reluctantly or under compulsion, for God loves a cheerful giver. [8] And God is able to make all grace abound to you, so that having all sufficiency in all things at all times, you may abound in every good work.

Paul also wrote to the Philippians encouraging them that the Lord would supply all their needs through Jesus and, according to His abundant riches in the heavenlies (Philippians 4:19).

Realize that in the above passages, apostle Paul includes material possessions among the things that the Lord gives. Therefore, we should think of material prosperity as part of God's grace, which He intends to stretch out to His church so that we can, in turn, do His work and help those in need.

- In 3 John 1:2, the apostle John prayed for the prosperity of a fellow believer named Gaius. He desired that Gaius might prosper and be in health, just as Gaius' soul was prospering.

Said in another way, John's prayer was that the prosperity of Gaius' soul (which means the salvation of his soul) would extend to all areas of Gaius' life.

John's Spirit-inspired prayer for Gaius applies to all believers since God does not show favoritism (Romans 2:11).

• It is never in God's perfect will to include those who are faithful to Him in judgments such as famine, which essentially means lack.

A good example is in the book of Revelation, where great scarcity follows the angelic rider on the black horse. In the passage, the price of a quart of wheat is so high (a day's wages) because there is a shortage. However, the command of God is clear: don't touch the wine and oil (Revelation 6:5-6).

What do wine and oil represent?

Those who have accepted Jesus Christ into their hearts have their sins cleansed through His blood, which is represented by wine (Matt 26:17-30). The Holy Spirit, symbolized by oil (Matthew 25:7-8), comes to dwell in the believer as a guarantee of salvation. Therefore, the wine and oil represent the church, the Body of Christ.

• The prophetic passages about the close of this age are evidence that it is God's perfect will that His children live in abundance.

The Bible says that during the millennial kingdom, we will have a taste of how the Lord intended the earth to be. God will perfect the world to be like it was before the fall of Adam.

One of the things that will mark that age will be abundance. There will be no hunger or thirst. And poverty will be a thing of the past. (The same will be the case in the new Heaven and Earth.)

In summary, great abundance is part of God's work of restoration that will take place in the new age (Revelation

7:13-17, Revelation 21:14-21, Psalm 132:13-16).

God's Nature

God's nature is always to bless. Since it is His nature, He can't help but bless! That means that His blessings will inevitably accompany His presence in our lives.

We see this throughout the Scriptures, including in Exodus 20:24, where God promised to bless anyone who would come to fellowship with Him at the altar.

In another example, the presence of God in Obed-Edom's life brought so much blessing that everyone noticed!

The Bible says, "[11] The ark of the Lord remained in the house of Obed-Edom the Gittite three months. And the Lord blessed Obed-Edom and all his household. [12] Now it was told King David, saying, "The Lord has blessed the house of Obed-Edom and all that *belongs* to him, because of the ark of God." So David went and brought up the ark of God from the house of Obed-Edom to the City of David with gladness." (2 Samuel 6:11-12)

As a point of clarification, the altar is the place of meeting between God and His people. And the ark is His dwelling place.

In the New Covenant, our bodies are the temple of God. The Lord dwells in our spirits (1 Corinthians 3:16). Therefore, we meet Him every time we come before Him in spirit and truth (John 4:24).

All in all, the presence of God that brought blessings to those in the Old Covenant will do the same for the Body of Christ in the New Testament since the Lord dwells with us and in us.

God is Good!

One of my favorite scriptures along this line is Psalm 81:13-16 (ESV), which says,

> 13 Oh, that my people would listen to me,
> that Israel would walk in my ways!
> 14 I would soon subdue their enemies
> and turn my hand against their foes.
> 15 Those who hate the Lord would cringe toward him,
> and their fate would last forever.
> 16 But he would feed you with the finest of the wheat,
> and with honey from the rock I would satisfy you.

It is incredible to read how God longs to show His goodness to His people. Realize that in the above passage, the Lord's perfect will was to feed His people with the finest of wheat and satisfy them with honey from the rock. He lamented the disobedience of Israel, which brought them destruction instead of His blessings.

Finally, we should always remind ourselves that God loves His people. When we study His dealings with humanity from Adam and Eve, to the patriarchs, Israel, and the church, we see that He cares about every aspect of our lives. The Lord is eager and delighted to show us His goodness by meeting our every need.

7. Heritage of the Righteous

One of our unique privileges as children of God is that we have access to the riches of our Father in heaven. Jesus taught us not to lose peace about what we are to eat or wear. Instead, we should focus on the kingdom of God and His righteousness because Abba cares for us. God knows what we need and is more than willing to provide (Matthew 6:31-34).

As God's people, we need to realize how much our Father is willing to do for us who love Him.

One of the most striking, thought-provoking, and faith-inspiring scriptures is Romans 8:31-32:

It is exciting to think about how God, the Almighty Creator of the universe, is for us. He is not against us. He loves us so much that He gave us Christ, His only begotten Son. There's no greater thing which God could have done to prove His love for us than the sacrifice of Jesus at the Cross.

Jesus Christ is the image or representation of the Father. Therefore, when the Father gave us Christ, He gave us Himself. Nothing can beat that!

Since God gave us the greatest thing He could have, His willingness to provide everything else pales in comparison. Providing for the material needs of His children pales in comparison. Driving out Satan pales in comparison. Healing our frail bodies pales in comparison. Creating new body parts pales in comparison. Guiding us in every decision pales in comparison. Everything else pales in comparison!

Our God is Good. We who honor Him, have faith in Him, and seek Him will be blessed. The Bible is clear that abundant provision is the heritage of the righteous.

That message is a central theme in the book of Psalms. For example:

• Psalm 34:8-10 declares that we should taste and see how good God is. The scripture assures us that blessings are upon those who trust in the Lord. The Psalm urges us to honor Him greatly. Those who do so will not lack. Even the young lions, children of the rulers of the jungle, do lack sometimes. But, those who seek God will not be deficient in any good thing.

• The Psalmist declares how the Lord is a sun and shield. He will give us grace and glory. Yes, He will not withhold any good thing from those who live a life full of love and holiness (Psalm 84:11).

• Psalm 35:27 says that God delights in the prosperity of His servants.

In addition to the Psalms, the book of Proverbs also brings this message home. God's perfect will for the righteous is that they have an abundance of everything they need:

• Proverbs 10:3 says that God won't allow those who live according to His word to be famished. On the other hand, He refuses to grant the desires of those who live wickedly.

• Proverbs 28:20 notes that those who are faithful will have many blessings. However, those who use devious means in their quest to quickly get rich will fall into trouble.

- It is also written in Proverbs 15:6 that there's much treasure in the house of the righteous, but in the revenue of the wicked is trouble.

8. Poverty

Poverty came through sin. Man first experienced what it means to be poor after Adam and Eve fell. That's when the curse of sin that changed everything about the world began.

Initially, everything was perfect. The word of God describes a world that was full of beauty, abundance, and the goodness of God (Genesis 1&2). Moreover, Adam and Eve were to work in the Garden of Eden and enjoy the fruit of their labor (Genesis 2:8-17).

Oppression entered the earth after the first man and woman sinned. God told them that the ground had been cursed because of their disobedience. For the first time, Adam and Eve would face a situation where they would struggle to make ends meet. They would labor but not see the fruit of their labors as they should.

The Bible notes God's exact words in Genesis 3:17-19:

> 17 Then to Adam He said, "Because you have heeded the voice of your wife, and have eaten from the tree of which I commanded you, saying, 'You shall not eat of it':
>
> "Cursed *is* the ground for your sake;
> In toil you shall eat *of* it
> All the days of your life.
> 18 Both thorns and thistles it shall bring forth for you,

And you shall eat the herb of the field.
[19] In the sweat of your face you shall eat bread
Till you return to the ground,
For out of it you were taken;
For dust you *are,*
And to dust you shall return."

The curse of poverty began to operate from that time onwards. It became more severe as sin increased. For instance, the Lord said that poverty would oppress Cain more heavily because he had sinned even more by killing his brother Abel.

Genesis 4:10-12 records, "[10] And He said, "What have you done? The voice of your brother's blood cries out to Me from the ground. [11] So now you *are* cursed from the earth, which has opened its mouth to receive your brother's blood from your hand. [12] When you till the ground, it shall no longer yield its strength to you. A fugitive and a vagabond you shall be on the earth."

Cain cried out to God because of the repercussions of his sin. In Genesis 4:13, he pleaded that they were too much for him to bear.

Unfortunately for Cain, there was no remedy for sin at that time — the forgiveness of sin and the cancellation of its effects came with Jesus Christ. Therefore, the consequences of his sin had to follow him wherever he went. Nevertheless, God in His mercy placed His mark of protection over Cain so that no one could harm him (Genesis 4:14-15).

Sin continued throughout the Old Covenant. The sins of the forefathers and fathers right from Adam continued to affect the children even though the children were not guilty of their parents' evil (Deuteronomy 28, Ezekiel 8).

Subsequent generations added on their wickedness and then passed the effects on to their children. As evil continued, the curse of sin became worse. Death, destruction, and poverty continued. Sin and the curse of sin became a cycle that grew stronger and stronger over humanity.

We see that pattern in the lives of the Israelites. A process of restoration of every aspect of their lives would begin whenever they served God. Israel would be blessed in every way as their relationship with the Lord grew stronger. And the blessings of God would increase as long as they shunned sin (Deuteronomy 28).

The converse would happen to Israel whenever sin increased in any generation. Poverty would come in. Deuteronomy 28:15-68 predicted that things would get worse and worse to a point where Jerusalem would lack even the most basic needs.

Talking about the same issue, the writings of the prophets warned that immense poverty would come as a result of disobedience:

Isaiah prophesied,

> **3** For behold, the Lord God of hosts
> is taking away from Jerusalem and from Judah
> support and supply,
> all support of bread,
> and all support of water; (Isaiah 3:1, ESV)

The prophet Jeremiah shared the same message that

iniquity (which means sin and its consequences) would withhold good from Israel. The land would go through a period of drought because of the sins of the inhabitants (Jeremiah 5:24-25).

Old Testament Language

It is necessary to clarify the language used in the Old Testament because calamities are at times attributed to God.

For example, Isaiah 45:7 reads,

> 7 I form the light and create darkness,
> I make peace and create calamity;
> I, the Lord, do all these *things.*

Addressing this is very important because an inadequate understanding of the Old Testament and its language has resulted in some falling into the error of accepting tragedy as God's will.

How many times have we heard of a good person who is genuinely committed to Jesus take poverty, sickness, or any other trouble as being from the Lord? On the other end, some unbelievers have rejected God because they have great difficulty reconciling the truth that He is Love yet He causes calamities.

We need to realize that the Old Covenant picture of God and His works was not complete because there was no understanding of Satan. A full understanding of the devil and his works came with the teaching and ministry of Jesus Christ (1 John 3:8).

So then, **the Old Testament is accurate but not complete**. In other words, as in the scripture above, the Old

Testament focuses on one side of the picture, that God is the Supreme Ruler of the universe.

Because God is Supreme, the reality is that nothing can happen without Him allowing it. However, we should not forget that there are reasons why God would allow a calamity to come upon a person or a group of people.

The good news is that the Bible explains itself. Therefore, to understand this view, let's go back to the Scriptures:

The book of Job is one of the few Old Testament books which identifies Satan explicitly and describes his works clearly.

While reading the passage below, pay attention to Satan's language when he came before God a second time to request permission to attack Job's body.

Job 2:4-5 says, "4 So Satan answered the Lord and said, "Skin for skin! Yes, all that a man has he will give for his life. 5 But stretch out Your hand now, and touch his bone and his flesh, and he will surely curse You to Your face!"

Did you notice that **Satan asked God to stretch out His hand and attack Job's body?** Pause for a moment. Who attacked Job's body? Was it God or Satan?

Job 2:6 records God's response to Satan's request: "6 And the Lord said to Satan, "Behold, he *is* in your hand, but spare his life.""

That response is interesting because it proves that **God understood Satan to be asking for His permission before attacking and not Him to cause harm to Job**. That means that **the Old Testament equates God allowing the attack to proceed to God being the cause**.

The Complete Picture

A more thorough understanding of why poverty and other misfortunes exist is that **Satan and his agents of all kinds of oppression have the authority to operate because humanity chose to sin.**

God gave the earth to mankind but then we invited the devil through our sin. Therefore, the Lord had no option but to allow Satan to operate on the planet even though the enemy's desire has been and will always be to steal, kill, and destroy (John 10:10).

The Father, on the other hand, is a good God. And, He does not delight in the suffering of people. Everything He created was good and perfect (Genesis 1&2). To reiterate, poverty and other misfortunes were never in the perfect will of God.

Was Jesus Poor?

There's always a debate about whether Jesus was rich or poor whenever the topic of money comes up in the church. Many wonder what the Bible means in 2 Corinthians 8:9, where it says that Jesus was made poor.

To begin with, to be rich means to have enough wealth to take care of ourselves and also to help those around us.

It is clear that Jesus did not sleep hungry. He had an abundance of everything through natural and supernatural means. Jesus had unlimited access to the grace of God:

- When Jesus needed to feed the multitudes, He multiplied food and drink numerous times (Matt 14:13-21, Matt 15:29-39, John 2:1-11).

• When He needed to pay taxes, He sent Peter to get money from the mouth of the fish (Matthew 17:24-27).

• When the disciples didn't catch any fish, twice, He made fish appear miraculously. The fish was so much that the apostles struggled to drag it into their boats (Luke 5:1-11, John 21:1-14).

• When He needed a room for His Last Supper with the disciples, He sent Peter and John to a house that had been miraculously prepared (Luke 22:8).

• In addition to all these supernatural works, the women who followed Him also supported His ministry financially (Luke 8:1-3).

The above examples demonstrate that the Lord had an abundance of everything He ever needed. So then, when did Jesus Christ become poor? The answer is, at the Cross.

At the Cross, the Son of God lacked the most basic things: He was thirsty, and He was naked (Matt 27:35, John 19:28). Therefore, the Lord experienced what it means to be the poorest of the poor.

While on that Cross, Jesus Christ was the poor Lamb of God crucified for our sin. On that day, He tasted the effect of the sin He was taking away from us.

Humility vs. Poverty

In conclusion, it is crucial to distinguish between humility and poverty. The Lord lived humbly by becoming a Man. He, however, was never poor until the Cross.

Some have elevated poverty because, in their eyes, the two are the same – to be poor is to be humble, and to be humble is to be poor. That view, however, can't be farther from the truth. There are prideful poor people and humble rich people.

However, a poverty-stricken person is indeed more likely to be humble because of their struggles, which typically make them realize that they need help.

Jesus Defeated Poverty

The good news is that Jesus Christ came to undo sin and all its effects. That includes poverty since it is one of the effects of sin that began after the fall in Genesis.

In fact, 2 Corinthians clearly states that one of Christ's intentions was to deliver us from poverty.

The passage reads, "[9] For you know the grace of our Lord Jesus Christ, that though He was rich, yet for your sakes He became poor, that you through His poverty might become rich." (2 Corinthians 8:9)

Another book that testifies to this truth is the prophecy of Isaiah. According to the writings of the prophet, being delivered from hunger and thirst is part of being taken out of prison:

Isaiah 49:8-10 (ESV) declares,

> 8 Thus says the Lord:
> "In a time of favor I have answered you;
> in a day of salvation I have helped you;
> I will keep you and give you
> as a covenant to the people,
> to establish the land,
> to apportion the desolate heritages,
> 9 saying to the prisoners, 'Come out,'

to those who are in darkness, 'Appear.'
They shall feed along the ways;
on all bare heights shall be their pasture;
10 they shall not hunger or thirst,
neither scorching wind nor sun shall strike them,
for he who has pity on them will lead them,
and by springs of water will guide them."

In other words, the salvation that Jesus provides includes deliverance from the bondage of poverty.

9. The Love of God

What drives God to act? What makes Him pay attention to every detail of our lives? Simply, why does God care?

The motivating force for God has been and will always be His love. God does everything, including providing for material needs, because He is gracious and full of compassion.

Psalm 36:7-10 declares,

> 7 How precious *is* Your lovingkindness, O God!
> Therefore the children of men put their trust under the shadow of Your wings.
> 8 They are abundantly satisfied with the fullness of Your house,
> And You give them drink from the river of Your pleasures.
> 9 For with You *is* the fountain of life;
> In Your light we see light.
> 10 Oh, continue Your lovingkindness to those who know You,
> And Your righteousness to the upright in heart.

When we love someone, naturally, we want them to prosper. Similarly, God wants the best for all of us. He rejoices over His people and wants all of us to thrive.

It is God's love that compels Him to act when He sees His people in any trouble. We learn this from Israel's case, where He would send messengers to deliver them every time they got themselves into problems.

Judges 2:16-18 narrates how Israel went through a cycle of falling into idolatry. The nation would end up falling into subjugation as a result. God would pity them when He saw how much they were struggling under the weight of oppression. He would then anoint a judge with a special grace to deliver Israel.

It is worth noting that although this happened numerous times, God never stopped loving Israel. Not just Israel, He has never stopped loving the entire world!

It is that same love that made Him send His Son to the Cross. We were all sinners destined to die forever. But, God in His compassion had a solution, Jesus Christ.

Jesus loved us to the end and took our place at the Cross. In the greatest demonstration of love, He became accursed at the Cross even though He had no sin so that He could free us from the curse of the Law (John 13:1, John 15:13).

Instead of curses, we receive the blessing of Abraham and the promise of the Holy Spirit through Jesus Christ (Galatians 3:13). We are blessed in all things (Genesis 24:1).

In Deuteronomy 30:9-10, the word of God says, "9 The Lord your God will make you abound in all the work of your hand, in the fruit of your body, in the increase of your livestock, and in the produce of your land for good. For the Lord will again rejoice over you for good as He rejoiced over your fathers, 10 if you obey the voice of the Lord your God, to keep His commandments and His statutes which are written in this Book of the Law, *and* if you turn to the Lord your God with all your heart and with all your soul."

The truth of the matter is that that promise applies to all of God's people since He is Just. He has no favorites (Isaiah 56). The promise of abundant financial provision is ours because of the love of the Father!

10. Living Testimonies

As Christians, we continuously encounter many questions about our faith in Jesus. Questions like, "If your God is real, then why are you struggling with your finances?" often come up as a challenge to our faith. Some practically-minded people have disregarded the message of the Gospel of Jesus Christ because they don't see how Christians can claim to serve the true God, yet, in some cases, believers are worse off financially.

Should we disregard these questions? What does the Bible say about God's intention to use our lives as testimonies to those who don't believe in Him so that they can perhaps change their minds? Is there a possibility that God desires to use His financial blessings (among other things) as a means to prove that He is God? Did Jesus ever provide for people as a means to draw them to Himself? Finally, where should we draw the line between seeking God for the sake of gaining money and material provision being a sign that God is real?

Let's examine the ministry of the Lord. In the Gospel of John, Jesus fed a great multitude of more than five thousand people and then traveled to another town on the other side of the sea. The people he had fed pursued Him zealously until they found Him. The Lord spoke to them in John 6.

Jesus revealed what was going on in their hearts when He

said, "[26] ... Most assuredly, I say to you, you seek Me, not because you saw the signs, but because you ate of the loaves and were filled." (John 6:26)

The language the Lord used is essential. He must have been including the miraculous sign of multiplying bread when He used the word 'signs'. Realize that He could have performed other signs, but He singles this out as the one that was so profound for the multitude that they ended up following Him wherever He went.

The fact that He referred to His multiplying of food as one of the 'signs' means that His material provision was not an end to itself since signs should indicate or direct us to something.

No doubt, the crowd was hungry, and so He fed them. However, His ability to multiply food was intended to open their eyes to the fact that He was the Son of God and the Savior they were waiting for. He pointed out that He is the real 'Bread from Heaven' and not the bread they had just eaten (John 6:33-34).

In that portion of Scripture, the Lord was essentially saying that 'I provided for you because you were hungry, but you shouldn't follow Me just because I can meet your material needs. My miraculous provision is a sign to you that I am the Messiah. My provision should help you believe that I am Your Savior. I care about your needs, and I will provide for you. But, the main goal of My provision is to prove to you that I am the Son of God'.

Therefore, the above instance is an example of God providing for the material needs of people as a way of drawing them to salvation.

Israel's Example

God's dealings with Israel also demonstrate His intention to use every means, including material or financial provision, to draw people to Himself.

Jeremiah 33:8-9 (ESV, emphasis added) reads, "[8] I will cleanse them from all the guilt of their sin against me, and I will forgive all the guilt of their sin and rebellion against me. [9] **And this city shall be to me a name of joy, a praise and a glory before all the nations of the earth who shall hear of all the good that I do for them. They shall fear and tremble because of all the good and all the prosperity I provide for it**."

Thus, the last part of the passage above emphasizes that the whole earth would stand in awe of God when they hear about the good that He would do to Israel. In other words, Israel would be forgiven, restored, and greatly blessed so much that the whole earth would honor God when they see what He has done.

The prophet Zephaniah shares a similar message in a prophecy about the restoration of Israel.

Zephaniah 3:20 (ESV, emphasis added) says,

[20] At that time I will bring you in,
at the time when I gather you together;
for I will make you renowned and praised
among all the peoples of the earth,
when I restore your fortunes
before your eyes," says the Lord.

Lastly, Psalm 67:1-3,7 (emphasis added) makes this point very clear. In the passage, the Psalmist declares:

67 God be merciful to us and bless us,
And* cause His face to shine upon us, *Selah
2 That Your way may be known on earth,
Your salvation among all nations.
3 Let the peoples praise You, O God;
Let all the peoples praise You...
7 God shall bless us,
And all the ends of the earth shall fear Him.

In conclusion, it is God's will that His people be a light to the world in every way. Isaiah 60:1-5 reveals that the nations of the world are supposed to look up to God's covenant people because of the manifestation of the glory of the Lord in our lives. When we have this mindset, we will want our lives to be instruments in God's hands in this way!

11. Christian and Lacking

God desires that there should be no poverty among His people. Nevertheless, it is clear from the Bible that there would be situations where some would struggle financially. That means that, although poverty is not ideal, a Christian could be impoverished.

In my opinion, nowhere in the Bible is this truth more explicitly expressed than in the book of Deuteronomy, which records Moses' final speech to Israel.

In the book, the servant of God instructed the nation on what to do and expect when they finally possess the fertile land that the Lord had promised to give to the descendants of Abraham hundreds of years before in Genesis 15:12-20.

Israel was finally at the border of the Promised Land. They had spent 40 years wandering in the desert until the generation that didn't believe God's promise died (Numbers 14:20-25). That generation had refused to go into the good and prosperous land for fear of the giants despite the Lord's assurances that He would be with them (Numbers 13).

In that instance in the Bible, the new generation was listening as Moses revealed the heart of God concerning them. Numerous times, the Lord reminded Israel through the prophet that they were coming into prosperity as He had promised. God desired that they would continue to be blessed in every way, including materially, as they continued to obey Him (Deuteronomy 28).

When we read Deuteronomy 15:1-6, it is clear that God wanted His people to be so financially prosperous that they would be lenders and not borrowers. That means that, ideally, no Israelite should have been lacking.

The Lord, however, acknowledged that this would not always be the case. There would be instances where some Israelites would lack. In fact, God went further and designated the year of Jubilee to relieve the destitute from financial troubles.

In that year, all debts would be forgiven. There would be a reset of everyone's finances and a chance for all the Israelites to start their lives anew.

Moreover, God devised a second system to help the poor. He instructed Israel to remember the needy during harvest:

In Leviticus 19:9-10, the Lord told the Israelites not to harvest the entire yield. He commanded them to leave the corners of their fields untouched. In addition, they were not to go back to gather the leftovers of the vineyards or farmlands that they, for some reason, had forgotten to pick. In so doing, the poor and the immigrants could have something to eat.

Thus, it is clear that some of God's people would be poor even though it is God's perfect will that we should not be poverty-stricken (John 12:8, Deuteronomy 15:11).

That said, our attitude should always be to strive for the best that God has to offer. Yes, we should strive for a life of abundance. We should understand that we are children of the Most High God.

The book of Isaiah reminds us that the Lord cares and wants to deliver us out of poverty.

Isaiah 41:17-20 (ESV) says,

17 When the poor and needy seek water,
and there is none,
and their tongue is parched with thirst,
I the Lord will answer them;
I the God of Israel will not forsake them.
18 I will open rivers on the bare heights,
and fountains in the midst of the valleys.
I will make the wilderness a pool of water,
and the dry land springs of water.
19 I will put in the wilderness the cedar,
the acacia, the myrtle, and the olive.
I will set in the desert the cypress,
the plane and the pine together,
20 that they may see and know,
may consider and understand together,
that the hand of the Lord has done this,
the Holy One of Israel has created it.

Having understood what the Lord's will concerning our finances is, we need to act whenever there's a gap between the reality of our lives and the promises of God's word. When we find ourselves in poverty, we need first to believe that Jesus can take us out and then strive for the fulfillment of His promises through fasting, prayer, and obeying the word of God (which commands a lifestyle of diligence, among other things) until the Lord changes our situation. God is faithful. And He will get us out of poverty.

Finally, we need to be careful not to fall into covetousness.

We should keep Hebrews 13:5-6 in mind as we seek the Lord to break the bondage of poverty from our lives. We are to appreciate what we already have and give thanks to God while continuing to exercise our faith for Him to get us out of our financial troubles.

Faith

Faith comes first because it is impossible to please the Lord if we don't have it. The Bible says that those who come to Him must have faith that He is the answer to everything and that He responds to those who earnestly seek Him (Hebrews 11:6).

We need to believe that our God is able and willing to deliver us out of poverty. We need to have faith that we will see His goodness, just like David did during difficult moments of his life.

The king wrote,

> 13 *I would have lost heart,* unless I had believed
> That I would see the goodness of the Lord
> In the land of the living.
> 14 Wait on the Lord;
> Be of good courage,
> And He shall strengthen your heart;
> Wait, I say, on the Lord! (Psalm 27:13-14)

Our God can do the impossible. Psalm 107:35-38 says:

> 35 He turns a wilderness into pools of water,
> And dry land into watersprings.
> 36 There He makes the hungry dwell,
> That they may establish a city for a dwelling place,
> 37 And sow fields and plant vineyards,
> That they may yield a fruitful harvest.

38 He also blesses them, and they multiply greatly;
And He does not let their cattle decrease.

Moreover, 1 Samuel 2:7-8 declares that the Lord makes one rich or poor. He lifts or brings low. God elevates the beggar from the ash heap, which is a very lowly place, and then makes him sit among the rulers. The Lord is able to make the poor inherit elevated positions.

1 Chronicles 29:12 says that both riches and honor come from God. The Lord rules over all things. Furthermore, power and might are in His hand. God is able to give strength and make someone great.

Lastly, the Lord wants to demonstrate His power in the lives of those who believe in Him (2 Chronicles 16:9a). Consequently, He will deliver all of us from poverty if we can exercise our faith in Him.

Prayer and Fasting

The Lord Jesus Christ taught His disciples to bring all their requests to Abba, our Father in heaven (Matthew 6:9-13). The word of God assures us that the Lord will provide all our needs when we ask Him.

To emphasize, it is scriptural to pray for financial blessings. There are Biblical examples of this:

• In Psalm 118:25, the Psalmist prayed to God to prosper him. He requested,

25 Save now, I pray, O Lord;
O Lord, I pray, send now prosperity.

• The famous prayer of Jabez in 1 Chronicles 4:10 is a prayer asking God for prosperity:

> 10 And Jabez called on the God of Israel saying, "Oh, that You would bless me indeed, and enlarge my territory, that Your hand would be with me, and that You would keep *me* from evil, that I may not cause pain!" So God granted him what he requested.

We can be sure that when we meet Him in prayer (and fasting), we will discover like Abraham did that God provides (Genesis 22:14).

Lastly, Hosea 12:4 notes that Jacob struggled with the Angel and prevailed. Similarly, we should make up our minds to continue fighting until we receive all the blessings that God intends to give us (Genesis 32:22-30).

Breaking Demonic Oppression

There's no limit to what Satan targets. The Lord made it crystal clear that the devil intends to steal, kill, and destroy (John 10:10).

In Satan's view, anything is a prime target as long as he can inflict pain in a person's life. Therefore, it makes sense that finances is one of the areas that the devil focuses his attacks. Obviously, if a person's financial resources are limited, that person is also restrained in how much they can support the work of God, help themselves, and help others.

Spirits of Poverty

A perfect example that proves that Satan attacks finances, or there is such a thing as a spirit of poverty, is the story of Job.

The Bible explicitly says that Satan came before God to ask for permission to attack because there was no open door in Job's life (read more about this in Chapter 13). After God granted the request, Satan unleashed a wave of attacks that dramatically brought Job down from abundance to poverty.

The attacks came through robbers, natural disasters, and supernatural events like fire from the sky consuming Job's sheep and servants (Job 1:13-19).

Given that demons can and do attack finances, there's need to be free from every demonic influence before we can walk in the fullness of the blessings that God has for us. If we are not free from spirits of poverty, then, no matter what we do, Satan will always find a way to consume our financial resources.

It is a Biblical principle that freedom precedes possession of God's promises. If you think about it, it only makes sense that if we are trying to achieve something and there's an obstacle against us, then we have to remove that barrier before we can reach our goal.

The prophet Obadiah testifies to this principle in verse 17, where he wrote that there would be deliverance and holiness on Mt. Zion. Consequently, the house of Israel would possess everything that belongs to them.

In other words, sin and the enemies that came as a result of it would be removed so that the people of God can receive their blessings.

In another instance, the Psalmist prayed for God to deliver him from the hands of his enemies, who could be taken figuratively to represent the kingdom of Satan.

Psalm 144:11-15 says,

11 Rescue me and deliver me from the hand of foreigners,
Whose mouth speaks lying words,
And whose right hand *is* a right hand of falsehood—
12 That our sons *may be* as plants grown up in their youth;
That our daughters *may be* as pillars,
Sculptured in palace style;
13 *That* our barns *may be* full,
Supplying all kinds of produce;
That our sheep may bring forth thousands
And ten thousands in our fields;
14 *That* our oxen *may be* well laden;
That there be no breaking in or going out;
That there be no outcry in our streets.
15 Happy *are* the people who are in such a state;
Happy *are* the people whose God *is* the Lord!

Notice how the Psalmist recognized that deliverance from his enemies would translate to blessings to him and his children after him.

Fight for your Inheritance

Many Christians are happy to make it to heaven only. That, however, isn't the only thing God wants to do for us. We should not settle for less than everything Jesus intends to give us. We should oppose Satan until we receive our complete inheritance.

The book of Exodus gives us a good picture of this. In the book, Pharaoh, who symbolizes Satan and his kingdom, realized that he had to let the children of Israel go. The battle was fierce with God causing massive damage to Egypt through the plagues.

Realizing that he was losing the battle, Pharaoh tried to

hold on to as much as possible. He tried to get the children of Israel to give up their wealth. He bargained with Moses saying that they should take their children with them but leave their flocks and herds behind. (Exodus 10:24)

Moses, however, would have none of it.

In Exodus 10:26, he responded, saying, "[26] Our livestock also shall go with us; not a hoof shall be left behind. For we must take some of them to serve the Lord our God, and even we do not know with what we must serve the Lord until we arrive there."

Thus, Israel was not going to settle for anything less than the best. They were going to take with them everything that God intended. The nation was going to serve God with all they possessed.

We should have the same mindset. We must not relent until we receive all the blessings God desires for us to have!

Matters of the Heart

We should be careful not to fall into the trap of questioning God's love for us when we are going through economic hardship. There's a lot to learn from the exodus of Israel from Egypt to Canaan, which we could take to represent our journey from financial troubles to a place of abundance.

Some in the camp of Israel kept despairing and questioning God's love and intentions every time they faced a setback.

For example, Exodus 16:2-3 narrates, "[2] Then the whole congregation of the children of Israel complained against Moses and Aaron in the wilderness. [3] And the children of Israel said to them, "Oh, that we had died by the hand of the Lord in the land of Egypt, when we sat by the pots of meat *and* when we ate bread to the full! For you have brought us out into this wilderness to kill this whole assembly with hunger."

This attitude of questioning God's intentions and love is what the Bible calls 'tempting' or 'despising' God (Numbers 11:18-20).

As Christians, we should set our hearts and minds not to fall for it. Let us keep in mind that God is for us and not against us (Romans 8:31). He is not the author of troubles. As a matter of fact, He is the solution to our problems.

Habakkuk 3:17-19 declares that we should always rejoice in God even though the fig tree does not blossom, the vines do not produce any fruit, the olives fail, the fields yield no harvest, or we lose our flocks or herds (our properties). We should delight in God despite any misfortune we may face. We should always remember that the Lord is the God of our salvation. He will strengthen us, change our situations, and elevate us so that we walk in high places.

Our faith in God should be steadfast at all times. Through good seasons and bad seasons, we should continue trusting in God's love and goodness.

With that in mind, we should display the kind of maturity great servants of God showed when they faced difficulties:

- In 1 Samuel 30:6-8, David lost everything in an instant. He and his men had gone to battle and left their families and properties behind. When the army came back, they found that the Amalekites had raided them, kidnapped their families, and stolen their properties. It was a tough situation made worse when his men got angry with him and wanted to stone him.

Instead of complaining and becoming bitter against God, the Bible says that David strengthened himself in the Lord. He understood that God cared for him. He believed that the Lord was going to help him through the situation. Therefore, he sought His guidance. God assured him that if he pursued the raiders, he would recover all he had lost. David obeyed, and the Lord restored everything that the Amalekites had stolen from him and his army.

• Job honored God during the worst moment of his life. He refused to curse God, although he mistakenly thought that God, not Satan, was behind the calamities that had befallen him (Job 2:9-10, Job 6:8-10).

12. Wealth for the Kingdom

I once had a symbolic dream in which I saw members of a church, both men and women, dressed in various styles. All their clothes were a beautiful shade of purple. When the pastor asked for donations for a project aimed to win souls for the kingdom of God, the members contributed so much that it surprised the pastor. The church had more than enough for the work of the Gospel of Jesus Christ.

That dream was an illustration of a Biblical truth concerning finances. Since purple is the color of royalty or empowerment, the dream meant that God was going to empower His people to be able to partner with Him in demonstrating His love to the world.

Every time God wants to build His dwelling place, He empowers His people by making them prosperous so that they can contribute to His work.

All wealth belongs to God. In Haggai 2:8-9, the Lord said that all silver and gold is His and that He would provide for the building of His house. In the passage, God stated His desire to build a magnificent temple where all the nations would gather.

To illustrate, let us go back to the first house of God, the tabernacle of Moses.

The Lord had to make Israel wealthy before they could build the tabernacle. Psalm 105:37 recounts how He brought the Israelites out of Egypt with silver and gold. We get more details in Exodus 12:25-36, which narrates how Moses told the Israelites to ask the Egyptians to give them articles of silver, gold, and clothing. Because of God's favor, the Egyptians responded by handing over everything the Israelites asked.

Later, the Lord instructed Moses to ask everyone to willingly contribute towards the building of the tabernacle (Exodus 35:20-29). The Israelites responded enthusiastically. They contributed so much that at one point, Moses had to ask them not to give anymore because there was too much material for the work (Exodus 36:6-7).

A man after God's Heart

The Bible describes David as a man after God's heart (1 Samuel 13:14). That is because he always wanted to do God's will. He also had a strong desire to build the best temple for the Lord. However, God chose Solomon to do the job because David had shed blood in war (1 Chronicles 28:3).

In 1 Chronicles 22:5, we read how David noted Solomon's youth and inexperience and consequently made up his mind that he was going to make all the necessary preparations for the construction of the temple. The king was willing to help in whatever way he could while he was still alive because he understood that building the house of God, from the foundation to completion, required a lot of financial resources.

Together, the father and son embarked on the project. After they finished the preparations, the work began during King Solomon's rule (1 Chronicles 22:14-16, 1 Kings 5:17, 7:51).

When Solomon finally completed the temple, the structure was magnificent in every way. The fact that he overlaid the inside with gold gives us a glimpse of the splendor of this building (1 Kings 6:21). In his own words, King Solomon described the temple as an exalted house, a place in which God would dwell forever (1 Kings 8:12-13). God Himself recognized that Solomon had done his best when He attested to the fact that the temple was magnificent (2 Chronicles 7:21).

New Covenant Temples

In the New Testament, we believers in Christ are the temple of God. And the Father's heart is to see souls saved through Jesus Christ (John 3:16). Therefore, being a person after God's heart means determining to do God's work of building His temple in the lives of all humanity.

Preparing a place for God to dwell in means bringing souls to the kingdom. It also means teaching and equipping believers so that they can learn to demonstrate love to one another and the world.

It is worth stressing that there's nothing that takes preeminence in the mind of God than the spreading of the Gospel of His kingdom.

All of heaven has soul-winning as the number one priority. The salvation of souls is so precious to God that there's rejoicing in heaven when a single person comes to faith in Jesus Christ.

Let us not forget that growing the church requires significant financial resources the same way constructing the tabernacle and the two temples did. That is why we are to commit ourselves to contribute to this effort.

The Bible gives us precedence of this in the Gospel of Luke, where a group of women committed their finances to support the ministry of Jesus Christ and the work of the Gospel.

Luke 8:1-3 reads,

> **8** Now it came to pass, afterward, that He went through
> every city and village, preaching and bringing the glad
> tidings of the kingdom of God. And the twelve *were* with
> Him, 2 and certain women who had been healed of evil
> spirits and infirmities—Mary called Magdalene, out of
> whom had come seven demons, 3 and Joanna the wife of
> Chuza, Herod's steward, and Susanna, and many others
> who provided for Him from their substance.

Lastly, let us reckon that giving to the work of God is a practical demonstration of our love for God and people. Furthermore, when we contribute, more is given to us by the Lord so that we can continue to walk in His love. No doubt, God values those who support His work. For that reason, He promises to continue blessing those who give (Luke 6:38, Malachi 3:9-11).

Leading from the Front

God's model of leadership is leading by example. Therefore, church leaders should be among those who give even as they encourage others to do the same.

In the Scriptures, we find numerous examples of leaders devoted to God, who also dedicated their wealth to His work:

- During preparation for building the temple, the leaders

of Israel, both past and present, made contributions from their wealth.

In 1 Chronicles, we read that Israel's leaders, including Samuel the Seer, David himself, Saul, captains of the army, and the leaders of households devoted some of their wealth to the construction of the temple (1 Chronicles 26:26-28, 1 Chronicles 29:1-9).

- Josiah, one of the great kings of Judah, committed his wealth to make sure that the people celebrated Passover in the right way (2 Chronicles 35:7-10).
- The Israelites undertook the construction of the second temple after the exile in Babylon. In this instance as well, the leaders of the community dedicated their resources to the work of God (Ezra 2:68-69, Nehemiah 7:70-72).

13. Clash of Kingdoms

Any army needs funds to complete its mission of conquering and subduing the enemy. Therefore, victory in any war between two kingdoms boils down to the resources that each of the domains has at its disposal.

Similarly, both the kingdom of God and the kingdom of Satan need resources as they battle for lost souls.

It is in the interest of Satan to help those devoted to his work to acquire more resources while hindering resources from coming to the church. For that reason, **Satan employs every scheme he can to keep those who are devoted to God and His will in poverty**.

A good example of the devil's efforts to impoverish God's people is in the book of Judges:

Judges 6:1-6 narrates how the Midianites would wait until the Israelites had sown their farms before launching attacks. The Canaanites would descend on the land with massive numbers of livestock and camels that would eat all the produce and leave nothing behind. This mode of aggression would leave the Israelites with very little to feed themselves or their animals. Consequently, Israel was greatly impoverished and so cried out to the Lord for help.

Satan's Weapons

Satan's war against the prosperity of God's people continues today. To win this war, the church needs to understand the enemy's strategy and the weapons he uses. Furthermore, we need to realize that the devil prospers those who do his bidding.

To start, the Bible points us to the ant as an example to emulate in order to overcome poverty and have plenty.

Proverbs 6:6-11 (ESV) says,

> 6 Go to the ant, O sluggard;
> consider her ways, and be wise.
> 7 Without having any chief,
> officer, or ruler,
> 8 she prepares her bread in summer
> and gathers her food in harvest.
> 9 How long will you lie there, O sluggard?
> When will you arise from your sleep?
> 10 A little sleep, a little slumber,
> a little folding of the hands to rest,
> 11 and poverty will come upon you like a robber,
> and want like an armed man.

Notice that the ant is the epitome of what it means to be self-driven and have foresight, the result of which is plenty of food (riches).

Therefore, it makes sense that Satan, through the spirit of poverty, works in people's lives to produce laziness, procrastination, and a lack of foresight, all of which are opposites of the ant's positive attributes.

Actually, in Proverbs 23:19-21, the Bible explicitly mentions drunkenness, greed, and laziness as some of the weapons Satan uses to advance poverty.

1. Laziness

For our purposes, we can define laziness as an unwillingness to do any type of work. It is a mental attitude where a person never wants to engage in anything productive – be it building, solving, or creating anything.

The Order of God

The book of Genesis states that God originally intended that we work and take care of our sphere of influence (Genesis 2:15). We were supposed to enjoy the fruit of our labor and find satisfaction in our work the same way the Lord did when He looked at all that He had created and called it good (Genesis 1:31).

In God's design, work was supposed to be delightful and rewarding to man as he accomplished things on the earth with the help of the Lord.

Then, after finishing his work, man was supposed to renew himself by resting through sleep or relative inactivity of the mind and body.

The Order of Laziness

A lazy person does not find satisfaction in work. Instead, the sluggard corrupts the order God set by sleeping or being inactive most of the time. In that way, laziness is the exact opposite of the Lord's design on how we should function.

The Bible, especially in the book of Proverbs, preaches very sharply against laziness (Proverbs 10: 4-5, 23, 14:23, 19:15, 24, 20:13, 21:5).

God's word is so much against laziness that it commands that whoever does not work should not eat (2 Thessalonians 3:10).

Moreover, the word of God depicts laziness as the contrast

of being upright: Proverbs 15:19 says that the way of the lazy man is like a hedge of thorns, but the path of the upright is a highway.

That proverb implies that one can't be lazy and upright at the same time. That means that a lazy mindset is crooked — which is to say that laziness is not right in God's eyes!

Proverbs 18:9 communicates that a sluggish person is kindred to a great destroyer. This is because that person is wasting time instead of working or building. Another way to think about it is that since time is a resource, squandering it is equivalent to destroying.

Added to that, we need to recognize that laziness is a form of self-deception. Proverbs 26:16 says that the lazy man is wiser in his own eyes than seven smart people. Sooner or later, however, it dawns on the lazy person that they lost opportunities and made no progress in life when they occupied themselves with meaningless things (Proverbs 14:23). It is at that point that reality unmasks the self-deception of laziness.

Furthermore, the Bible is clear that laziness is contrary to the nature of God. It is against the Lord's instructions to mankind. And therefore, it has no place in the kingdom of God.

Lastly, we should emulate the Lord Jesus Christ in everything because He is the epitome of how the sons and daughters of God should operate. Jesus was very diligent in everything He did. He was always determined to complete every assignment that the Father gave Him. The Lord executed every instruction thoroughly and impeccably. In fact, finishing the Father's work is what gave Him satisfaction – in John 4:34, Jesus said that His food was to do God's will to completion.

2. Procrastination and Excuses

To procrastinate means to put off finishing a task until a later date. Such a mentality goes against God's approach to doing things because God is the God of 'Now'. The Lord does not want us to put off anything until tomorrow if we can do it today.

For example, it is His desire for all of us to be saved now. 2 Corinthians 6:2 says that now is the right time. Now is the time for salvation.

In addition, Proverbs 3:28 commands us not to tell our neighbor to come back tomorrow if we can immediately give them what they are seeking.

The problem with procrastination is that we may not get the opportunity to finish the task we are putting off for the simple reason that the future is never guaranteed.

On the contrary, a 'now' mentality means that we will probably complete the tasks we have to do because we will start working on them immediately.

In conclusion, laziness and procrastination are connected. If we are honest with ourselves, we will identify laziness as a major reason why we procrastinate on the assignments we need to complete.

Proverbs 24:30-34 says,

> 30 I went by the field of the lazy *man*,
> And by the vineyard of the man devoid of understanding;
> 31 And there it was, all overgrown with thorns;

Its surface was covered with nettles;
Its stone wall was broken down.
32 When I saw *it*, I considered *it* well;
I looked on *it and* received instruction:
33 A little sleep, a little slumber,
A little folding of the hands to rest;
34 So shall your poverty come *like* a prowler,
And your need like an armed man.

3. Greed

Greed means seeking to accumulate wealth by whatever means possible. Therefore, a greedy person will have no problem becoming prosperous at the expense of others.

That means that greed values riches more than it values the life of a human being. Strange as it seems, this may even include the life of the greedy person himself, although, in most cases, the greedy person doesn't recognize that they are harming themselves.

According to the Bible, one of the signs of greed is the lack of satisfaction with what one has – the greedy person will always want more to hoard for themselves.

For that reason, Ecclesiastes 5:10 notes that no amount of riches will satisfy us if we love money. No level of income will be enough for us if we love wealth.

The Bible warns us that the consequences of greed are enormous. The troubles that come because of this sin extend to the greedy person's family and everything he owns (Proverbs 15:27).

The trouble comes on both the spiritual and the natural level:

Take, for example, a couple engaging in dubious business practices to make more sales. That couple is engaging in habitual sin, which invites demonic activity. Because they also are parents, the generational effect of their sin extends to their children who know nothing about their activities (Deuteronomy 28). Thus, they will have brought trouble on themselves and their households on the spiritual level.

On the natural level, they may be breaking the law and could face imprisonment. Without a doubt, going to jail would affect them and their children.

Wealth Gained through Greed

There are important things to observe concerning wealth gained through greed:

First, riches gained through covetousness are temporary. They will eventually disappear (Proverbs 28:8, Jeremiah 17:11).

Secondly, wealth gained through greedy means may seem to be a blessing for a moment but will eventually become a curse. The irony is that the greedy person thinks they have earned, but they have lost in reality (Proverbs 20:17, Ezekiel 7:19).

Thirdly, such riches most certainly have no eternal value. On the contrary, since greed is sin, it leads to spiritual death (Proverbs 21:6, Proverbs 10:2, Proverbs 1:17-19).

In conclusion, greed is a trap of Satan. The enemy wants to use this trap against every Christian (as well as non-Christians). It is deceptive. It is sin.

If we take time to think about the consequences of wealth obtained through sin, we will quickly conclude that one would rather not have riches than gain it through ways that God does not approve. That is why the Bible says that it is better to have a little with righteousness than get a higher income without justice (Proverbs 16:8). We are much better off needy and righteous than rich and wicked (Proverbs 28:6). No amount of money is worth losing our souls!

4. Riches from Satan

As mentioned before, it is in the devil's interest to help those who further his purposes. Satan wants to enable those who knowingly or unknowingly do his will to continue doing so by helping them succeed in whatever evil they are carrying out.

People can and do gain riches from Satan directly or indirectly. By directly, I mean those who openly seek the devil's help to achieve prosperity. By indirectly, I mean those, such as drug dealers, who use sinful means to gain their wealth.

The following are two scriptural proofs that this can happen:

- The Bible teaches that after the fall of man, the devil gained authority over the earth and its resources. As a matter of fact, the Lord Jesus referred to the enemy as the ruler of the world in John 14:30.

Moreover, the Lord didn't refute as false Satan's claim that he had authority over the world during the temptation in the desert:

Luke 4:5-6 narrates that the devil took Jesus to a high mountain. He then instantly showed the Lord all the nations of the world. Satan claimed that he had authority over the kingdoms of the earth and their glory. He also said he could hand that authority to whomever he chose. The devil tried to entice Jesus to worship him in exchange for that authority, but the Lord refused. Jesus made it clear that the word of God commanded that man shall worship the Lord God only.

That said, it is worth noting that, at the Cross, Jesus defeated Satan. The enemy no longer has authority over anyone who has faith in Jesus Christ. The Bible says that the Lord transfers those who believe in Him from the reign of the kingdom of darkness into the realm of Light (Colossians 1:12-14).

• In Revelation 18:11-19, we read how those who were enriched by Satan's kingdom (symbolized by Babylon) will mourn when God finally destroys that kingdom from the face of the earth.

Futile

The Bible gives a stark warning to those who will seek to be enriched by Satan. Proverbs 10:22 says that the blessing of the Lord makes a person rich without adding any sorrows. Conversely, riches obtained through evil will bring sorrow and pain.

Furthermore, wealth gained unjustly through sin, or demonic power will flee.

Jeremiah 17:11 says,

> 11 *As* a partridge that broods but does not hatch,
> *So is* he who gets riches, but not by right;
> It will leave him in the midst of his days,
> And at his end he will be a fool.

Finally, Satan's aim has always been and will always be to steal, kill, or destroy (John 10:10). This is always true, including in situations where he pretends to be well-meaning by making a person wealthy. We should always recall that even if it seems for a moment that Satan is doing a desirable thing, his evil intentions will eventually unfold with time.

Why does God allow the wicked to prosper?

It is not surprising that Job had a lot of questions about the justice of God when he underwent a heavy barrage of vicious demonic attacks that reduced him to poverty and sickness (Job 21:17-21). Job was righteous, yet he was suffering while those living wickedly were prospering. How could that be?

In reality, these kinds of questions didn't end with Job. Many Christians still ask the same questions today. The answer as to why God allows the wicked to prosper remains complicated:

At the end of the book of Job, God responded to Job's complaints. The Lord made it clear that Job didn't fully understand the events that had taken place. Job's knowledge, like all of us, was minimal.

Job recognized his error in Job 40-42, where he noted that he had complained out of ignorance. The servant of God had talked about issues he didn't understand. He confessed that he had commented on things too grand for him to fathom. Job had realized that he didn't comprehend everything that God was doing from the beginning to the end after the Lord's questions left him dumbfounded.

The same is true for all of us. We don't know everything

God is doing. Yes, He reveals His plans to us step by step, but we never know everything from the beginning to the end. Moreover, every person is unique, and only God can reveal what He is doing in each person's life.

All in all, we can be sure that God is merciful and gives everyone a chance to repent from their lifestyle of sin (2 Peter 3:9). That partly explains His patience with those who are practicing evil. On our part, we must guard our hearts against envying those who are living wickedly and yet are prospering (Proverbs 23:17-18). Instead, we should be passionate about honoring God always. We have every reason to rejoice in God because there is a life after this earth, and those who hope in the Lord will not be disappointed.

Note on Job's Temptations

We later learn that Job's life and the attacks he went through were significant because they were a picture of the life of Jesus Christ (Job 1&2, Matthew 4, Luke 22&23):

• Job, like the Lord Jesus, lived a perfect and blameless life. Consequently, Satan had no access to their lives and had to get special permission from the Father to tempt and attack them directly.

• Satan was allowed to tempt Job to renounce his relationship with the Father on two occasions. The same thing happened to Jesus Christ – the temptation in the desert and the crucifixion.

• On the first occasion, the Father allowed the tempter to attack anything but Job's body. Likewise, the devil tempted the Lord in the desert but did not attack His body.

- In the second instance, the devil was allowed to attack Job's body. Similarly, he was granted permission to attack and kill the Lord through the crucifixion.

Therefore, even though Job didn't understand, his life mirrored the two major temptations the Lord faced at the beginning and end of His earthly ministry. Job's victory was a prediction that Jesus Christ would overcome the wiles of the enemy.

14. Seven Keys to Accumulating Wealth

Ecclesiastes 4:8 says,

> 8 There is one alone, without companion:
> He has neither son nor brother.
> Yet *there is* no end to all his labors,
> Nor is his eye satisfied with riches.
> *But he never asks,*
> "For whom do I toil and deprive myself of good?"
> This also *is* vanity and a grave misfortune.

In addition, Ecclesiastes 5:11 says that when goods increase, the number of those who eat them also increases. Therefore, accumulating too much to ourselves has no advantage except that it satisfies the eyes.

These two passages of Scripture are emphasizing to us that, first, we have to examine our intentions for wanting to create wealth. We must be very clear-headed about what we want to do with the financial resources we are trying to accumulate.

God's standard is apparent: Psalm 145:17-19 declares that He is righteous in everything He does. The Lord is gracious in all His works. He is near to those who pray to Him and close to those who call upon Him in truth. God will hear the cries of those who honor Him. He will save them and fulfill their desires.

Therefore, we can be sure that God will back us in our quest to acquire wealth when we are holy and our intentions pure, lovely, and good.

The Lord Jesus taught us that if we abide in Him and His words abide in us, we will ask what we desire, and He will do it for us. Note that abiding in Him includes obeying His commandment, which is love (John 15:7-10).

That means that if we want prosperity for the cause of love, then our hearts are right before God and we are doing a good thing. His answer to our requests will most likely be 'Yes'.

Secondly, we should recognize that God's will for each of us is different. We are all unique with distinct responsibilities in His kingdom. Consequently, we will inevitably have different levels of needs. This means that God will bestow upon each us different levels of prosperity depending on His will.

Although it is God's will that each of us has at least enough to supply our needs and help those around us, not all of us are destined to be the wealthiest person on earth. We should be wise enough to pray that God will grant us the amount of wealth that we can handle faithfully. Remember that at the end of the day, no amount of money is worth losing eternal life. The salvation of our souls comes first.

We have an example of such a clear-minded person in the book of Proverbs. Agur prayed that God would give him just enough – not too much that would make him forget God or too little that would make him steal from others.

Proverbs 30:7-9 (ESV, emphasis added) reads,

7 Two things I ask of you;
deny them not to me before I die:
8 Remove far from me falsehood and lying;
give me neither poverty nor riches;
feed me with the food that is needful for me,
9 **lest I be full and deny you**
and say, "Who is the Lord?"
or lest I be poor and steal
and profane the name of my God.

1. *Wisdom from God*

He received all the wealth that his father had apportioned to him. After journeying to a distant country, he was free to do as he pleased with his possessions. Far away from his father, he spent everything he owned without ever pausing to think about what would happen after the riches were gone.

His decisions landed him in poverty and shame. Eventually, his dire situation forced him to do what he should have done before – for the first time, he took a moment to think soberly about his decisions. His life took a right turn when he decided to humble himself and went back to his father, who lovingly accepted him. The father gave his son a chance to start all over again.

The story of the prodigal son presents us with the naked truth of what will eventually happen when we have riches but don't have wisdom (Luke 15:11-32).

The need for wisdom cannot be overemphasized. Happenings like that of the prodigal son are all around us today. The news media is full of stories of people who gained a lot of money through sports, music, and other professions but lost everything because they were not prudent.

Again and again, people fail to heed the warning of the word of God, which says, "Whoever loves wisdom makes his father rejoice, but a companion of harlots wastes *his* wealth." (Proverbs 29:3)

King Solomon is a prime example of a person who understood the value of wisdom. Faced with the daunting task of leading all of Israel, the young and inexperienced king knew how vital good judgment would be and so sought it from God (1 Kings 3:7-10).

Later, after God had given him an unprecedented level of wisdom, the wise king noted the preeminence of the same. He wrote that wisdom is better than weapons of war (Ecclesiastes 9:18).

Think about it. Wisdom is the greatest thing one could ever ask from the Lord. Nothing can take its place. Neither money nor gold can compare to it. The evidence of its superiority is that we could have many resources, but because we don't make the right decisions, those resources will go to waste.

The Best

To have wisdom is to know what to say or do in a given situation, including making financial decisions. That means that wisdom is relevant when we are facing a circumstance that requires us to choose between two or more options. Thus, when we ask God for wisdom, we are, in essence, asking Him to help us take the path that He would decide if He was facing the same situation.

God's direction is the best and most intelligent advice we could ever receive because it comes from His infinite and perfect knowledge of all things. If it is foolish not to hear the counsel of the wise, how much more foolish is it not to listen to the counsel of God? (Proverbs 12:15)

Finally, asking for wisdom delights God (1 Kings 3:11-15). It pleases God because it demonstrates that we are seeking the best outcome in every situation. The best result is that which is best for us and everyone else affected by the decisions we make, such as our families and the people looking up to us. In that sense, asking for wisdom is a demonstration of the love of God in our hearts.

Gaining Wealth through Wisdom

In many instances, the Bible correlates wisdom to wealth. The Scriptures tell us to seek the knowledge and understanding given by God. And riches will follow when we do so.

Proverbs 24:3-4 brings out this point. The scripture says that a house is built through wisdom, and by understanding it is established so that it stands firm. Through knowledge, the rooms of the house will be filled with riches.

Wisdom ranks higher than wealth because, through it, we will gain wealth plus more:

- Proverbs 3:13-15 says,

> 13 Happy *is* the man *who* finds wisdom,
> And the man *who* gains understanding;
> 14 For her proceeds *are* better than the profits of silver,
> And her gain than fine gold.
> 15 She *is* more precious than rubies,
> And all the things you may desire cannot compare with her.

- Proverbs 8:18-19 declares,

18 Riches and honor *are* with me,
Enduring riches and righteousness.
19 My fruit *is* better than gold, yes, than fine gold,
And my revenue than choice silver.

How to Get Wisdom for Finances

a) Supernatural Impartation

The Bible teaches us that God can impart wisdom in us supernaturally. Proverbs 2:6-7 says that the Lord gives wisdom. Knowledge and understanding come from His mouth. He is the defender of those who walk uprightly and stores up wisdom for them.

James, in his epistle, urges all of us to ask for wisdom from God. He notes that, because the Lord loves us, He will give it to us generously (James 1:5).

Since God wants us to make prudent financial decisions, we should pray to Him to impart His wisdom in us. Solomon, Daniel, and his three companions are examples of those to whom God supernaturally gave wisdom:

- 1 Kings 4:29-34 narrates how the Lord God gave Solomon wisdom and understanding that was exceedingly great. The king's insight into various issues surpassed that of all the men of the East and Egypt, two regions which, at the time, were known to have some of the wisest people.

The result of the unprecedented level of wisdom God gave Solomon was that the king spoke three thousand proverbs and composed one thousand and five songs. In his writings, King Solomon talked about various subjects like wisdom and the meaning of life. The king was so well regarded that people came from all over the earth just to hear him speak.

• The Bible says that God gave knowledge and skill in all literature and wisdom to Daniel, Hananiah, Mishael, and Azariah.

The king interviewed them at the end of their training and found none who could compare to the four. The Scripture says that the ruler found them to be ten times better than all the magicians and astrologers in every matter of wisdom and understanding about which he examined them. Consequently, they were assigned to work for the king (Daniel 1:17-20).

b) Knowledge and Experience

We also gain wisdom through our personal experiences and those of others who have gone through similar situations.

God designed the church and humanity as a whole such that we need each other. Therefore, we should not be ashamed to ask for help. It is to our advantage to talk to those who have succeeded as well as those who have failed because, through their experiences, we learn what to do or not.

Furthermore, we still need to be financially educated and trained even though we are Christians and have a relationship with God. Finances affect all of us and we will, at some point, need to make decisions concerning the same. So then, if we are to be good stewards, we need to have a thorough understanding of how financial systems work.

2. The Leading of the Spirit

It is necessary to hear the voice of God and be led by the Spirit. We continually need the advice of God in all things.

Jeremiah 10:23 (ESV, emphasis added) says,

> 23 I know, O Lord, that the way of man is not in himself,
> that **it is not in man who walks to direct his steps**.

God's guidance beats any counsel we could ever get from a man. It is above all the research we could ever do before making any decision or investing in any venture. Simply, nothing compares to the leading of the Lord!

The good news is that the Lord expects us to seek help from Him. He guarantees that when we seek Him, we will find Him. When we ask Him in faith, He will guide us:

- In Isaiah 48:17, He reminds us that He is the Lord who teaches us to profit. He is the God who directs us on which path we should take.

- Psalm 25:12-15 states that the Lord will teach those who fear Him. Those who stand in awe of God will dwell in prosperity, and their descendants inherit the earth. God shares His secrets with those who fear Him and shows them His faithfulness.

- In Isaiah 58:11 (ESV), the word of God promises those who fast in the right way that:

> 11 ... the Lord will guide you continually
> and satisfy your desire in scorched places
> and make your bones strong;

and you shall be like a watered garden,
like a spring of water,
whose waters do not fail.

In conclusion, the Bible promises us that our prosperity is guaranteed as long as we obey God's directions and continue in faith to the end. Speaking along this line, 2 Chronicles 26:5 gives us the example of King Uzziah about whom the Bible says that as long as he sought the Lord, God made him prosper.

3. Talents and Abilities

We should put the skills and abilities (graces) that God has given us to work. Excellent skills will no doubt bring favor. They are the means through which we will prosper:

- According to Proverbs 18:16, the gift of a man will make room for him. His talent will bring him before great men.

- Proverbs 22:29 says that a person who excels in their work will interact with kings. That person will not stand before unknown people.

Lastly, the world will always be willing to pay for exceptional talent just like in King Solomon's case. 1 Kings 10:24-25 narrates, "[24] Now all the earth sought the presence of Solomon to hear his wisdom, which God had put in his heart. [25] Each man brought his present: articles of silver and gold, garments, armor, spices, horses, and mules, at a set rate year by year."

4. Diligence

The Bible teaches us to work hard in everything we engage in, whether school, the workplace, or our businesses. The Scriptures are emphatic that industriousness brings wealth, while laziness leads to poverty:

- Proverbs 10:4-5 declares that the person with idle hands will become poor while those whose hands are diligent will become rich. Moreover, a child who gathers harvest during the summer is wise, while those who sleep in the reaping season are foolish.

- Proverbs 28:19 tells us that those who work their land will have plenty of food while those who chase fantasies instead of working hard will be full of poverty.

- Proverbs 20:4 notes that the lazy person makes an excuse not to plow, saying that it is the winter. Therefore, he will have to beg during the harvest because he will have nothing.

- Proverbs 12:11 reads,

> 11 He who tills his land will be satisfied with bread,
> But he who follows frivolity *is* devoid of understanding.

5. Self-Discipline and Sacrifice

We have to learn to make the necessary sacrifices if we are going to be prosperous. Self-discipline will be essential to meet the goals we set to achieve. For instance, saving requires self-control. We will end up destitute if we do not discipline ourselves enough to know when to deny ourselves and when to spend what we have.

The Bible warns that those who love pleasure will be poor. The person who loves wine and oil will not be wealthy (Proverbs 21:17). The word of God also says that there are treasures and oil in the house of the wise. However, a foolish man will waste those treasures (Proverbs 21:20).

Lastly, the Scripture in Proverbs 23:19-21 (ESV) admonishes,

19 Hear, my son, and be wise,
and direct your heart in the way.
20 Be not among drunkards
or among gluttonous eaters of meat,
21 for the drunkard and the glutton will come to poverty,
and slumber will clothe them with rags.

6. Being Strategic

24 There are four things which are little on the earth,
But they are exceedingly wise:
25 The ants are a people not strong,
Yet they prepare their food in the summer;
26 The rock badgers are a feeble folk,
Yet they make their homes in the crags;
27 The locusts have no king,
Yet they all advance in ranks;
28 The spider skillfully grasps with its hands,
And it is in kings' palaces.
– Proverbs 30:24-28 (emphasis added)

Through this proverb, we learn four valuable insights about accumulating wealth:

• From the ants, we learn about planning for the future: Ants store food at the right time (summer) so that they have enough to eat when the seasons become unfavorable.

• From the rock badgers, we learn to seek the help of those who are stronger: Rock badgers are weak, but they hide in rocks, which are strong. The lesson here is that we will always need help in life. The wisest thing to do is to recognize our weaknesses and then seek the assistance of those who are strong in the areas that we are inadequate.

One relevant application of this principle is investing. For example, we may not be knowledgeable about how to invest in stocks. However, we could ask a money manager with a proven track record to handle our finances in exchange for a fee.

• From the locusts, we learn how to work in teams and recognize our functions: These insects are successful because they are orderly. Each one knows its place.

That means we have to acknowledge that we can't be the best in everything. Consequently, we should be comfortable taking the lead in areas in which we are the best. And, in those areas where we are not, we should have the humility to let others lead and we follow.

For example, in building a business, an entrepreneur will need to assemble a team with various skill sets. The founder of the company may be very good at designing and creating products but not in sales. Therefore, he will have to rely on an employee who is better skilled at marketing to drive all the company's sales efforts.

• From the spiders, we learn that being very skillful will open doors for us in high places: Spiders are unique in that they use their skills to get into the quarters of royalty. Therefore, we should master and excel in the skills we have because it is those skills that will bring us before kings and earn us income. It is our expertise that will elevate us in life.

Note on Planning for the Future

Planning for the future is not a demonstration of a lack of

faith. It is a Biblical principle.

We have to be wise stewards of what we have. In the book of Proverbs, the Bible urges us to prepare for the future because we are never sure of everything that will happen. We don't have perfect knowledge of the future.

Proverbs 27:23-27 (ESV) advises,

> 23 Know well the condition of your flocks,
> and give attention to your herds,
> 24 for riches do not last forever;
> and does a crown endure to all generations?
> 25 When the grass is gone and the new growth appears
> and the vegetation of the mountains is gathered,
> 26 the lambs will provide your clothing,
> and the goats the price of a field.
> 27 There will be enough goats' milk for your food,
> for the food of your household
> and maintenance for your girls.

In Noah's story, we find a case where God Himself instructed a man to store up for the future because the flood would cause a season of hardship upon the earth (Genesis 6:21-22).

In another example, God warned Pharaoh through a dream about a coming famine that would affect all of Egypt and the surrounding nations. Joseph relied on the Spirit to interpret the dream and then acted on the warning by setting up storage units of grain during the years of plenty that preceded the great famine which impoverished most Egyptians (Genesis 41:28-36).

Pharaoh ended up owning all the land in Egypt because

he was prepared for the famine while the rest of the nation had to sell their properties to survive. As the famine impoverished everyone else, Pharaoh was selling grain and getting wealthier because he heeded the word of God. He had an advantage because he was prepared for the future (Genesis 47:18-26).

Finally, turning to the New Testament, Jesus and the apostles had a treasury where they kept their money for future use (John 13:29).

7. Take Calculated Risks

We have to take a measure of risk to achieve anything in life. Ecclesiastes 11:4-5 says, "He who observes the wind will not sow, and he who regards the clouds will not reap. As you do not know what the way of the wind is or how the bones grow in the womb of her who is with child, so you do not know the works of God who makes everything."

Knowing that risks are unavoidable, we have to mitigate them by spreading them out. Therefore, don't put all your eggs in one basket, try many things. Invest in many ventures:

- Ecclesiastes 11:6 (ESV) notes,

  6 In the morning sow your seed, and at evening withhold not your hand, for you do not know which will prosper, this or that, or whether both alike will be good.

- Isaiah 32:20 says,

  20 Blessed *are* you who sow beside all waters,
  Who send out freely the feet of the ox and the donkey.

- Proverbs 27:23-27 instructs us to,

23 Be diligent to know the state of your flocks,
And attend to your herds;
24 For riches *are* not forever,
Nor does a crown *endure* to all generations.
25 *When* the hay is removed, and the tender grass shows itself,
And the herbs of the mountains are gathered in,
26 The lambs *will provide* your clothing,
And the goats the price of a field;
27 *You shall have* enough goats' milk for your food,
For the food of your household,
And the nourishment of your maidservants.

15. God's Supernatural Provision

[28] So why do you worry about clothing? Consider the lilies of the field, how they grow: they neither toil nor spin; [29] and yet I say to you that even Solomon in all his glory was not arrayed like one of these. [30] ***Now if God so clothes the grass of the field, which today is, and tomorrow is thrown into the oven, will He not much more clothe you, O you of little faith****? [31] Therefore do not worry, saying, 'What shall we eat?' or 'What shall we drink?' or 'What shall we wear?' [32] For after all these things the Gentiles seek. For your heavenly Father knows that you need all these things. [33]* ***But seek first the kingdom of God and His righteousness, and all these things shall be added to you.***

–Matthew 6:28-33 (emphasis added)

In the passage above, the Lord stated that it is the Father's will to meet all of our needs as long as we fulfill these conditions which He laid out:

1. Have faith in God.
2. Seek the kingdom of God, which includes finding out and obeying the will of the Lord.
3. Live in holiness.

When we satisfy the above, we have every right to expect that the Father will provide for us. The pertinent question then becomes: what are the supernatural ways through which He provides?

1. Supernatural Increase of the Labor of our Hands

> [7] *For the Lord your* ***God has blessed you in all the work of your hand****. He knows your trudging through this great wilderness. These forty years the Lord your God has been with you; you have lacked nothing.*
> *– Deuteronomy 2:7 (emphasis added)*

From the scripture above, we learn that God can make His people prosperous by blessing the tasks in which we are engaged. The Lord wants to multiply the fruit of our labor. He desires to supernaturally increase the work of our hands.

Natural laws don't limit God. He can supernaturally multiply things and demonstrates throughout the Bible that He is more than willing to do that for His people.

For instance, as mentioned earlier, Isaac sowed in the land during drought and reaped in the same year a hundredfold because of the Lord's blessing (Genesis 26:12-14).

Moreover, Isaac's son Jacob experienced a similar supernatural increase of the herd he owned as pay from Laban (Genesis 31:7-12).

The Lord did it for the patriarchs, He did it for Israel, and He is willing to do it for His church.

In fact, on two occasions in the Gospels, Jesus did it for Peter and the other apostles when He enabled them to catch fish supernaturally:

> [4] And when he had finished speaking, he said to

> Simon, "Put out into the deep and let down your nets for a catch." [5] And Simon answered, "Master, we toiled all night and took nothing! But at your word I will let down the nets." [6] And when they had done this, they enclosed a large number of fish, and their nets were breaking. [7] They signaled to their partners in the other boat to come and help them. And they came and filled both the boats, so that they began to sink. (Luke 5:4-7, ESV)

> [5] Jesus said to them, "Children, do you have any fish?" They answered him, "No." [6] He said to them, "Cast the net on the right side of the boat, and you will find some." So they cast it, and now they were not able to haul it in, because of the quantity of fish. (John 21:5-6, ESV)

2. Supernatural Abilities

God can give us wisdom, skill, and knowledge to excel in every kind of work. He created all things and, therefore, can supply any ability as required.

Philippians 4:13 declares that we can do all things through Christ who strengthens us.

'All things' means all things! God can give us any talent or ability, according to His will. All we need to do is ask.

A case in point is in the book of Exodus, where God, through His Spirit, gave Bezalel the ability to work artistically on gold, silver, bronze, precious stones, and wood (Exodus 31:1-5).

Another example is David, who recognized that God had enhanced his fighting skills. He said in Psalms 18:31-34 (ESV) that:

31 For who is God, but the Lord?
And who is a rock, except our God?—
32 the God who equipped me with strength
and made my way blameless.
33 He made my feet like the feet of a deer
and set me secure on the heights.
34 He trains my hands for war,
so that my arms can bend a bow of bronze.

In Psalm 144:1 (ESV), the king of Israel praised the Lord saying,

144 Blessed be the Lord, my rock,
who trains my hands for war,
and my fingers for battle"

3. Favor

Favor is one of God's favorite instruments in prospering His people. God's favor upon a person's life will make others want to be kind to that person. It drives others to want to help us achieve whatever it is we are pursuing.

The following are instances where God's favor enabled His people to prosper:

• Joseph was protected from harm and promoted because of God's favor. After he had been sold into slavery by his siblings, Potiphar, who had bought him, favored him and made him the overseer of his house.

Later, Joseph was wrongfully accused of attempted rape and sent to prison. Even there, God gave him favor. Consequently, the keeper of the prison elevated Joseph to be the supervisor of all the prisoners (Genesis 39:3-5, 23).

Afterward, Pharaoh favored Joseph and promoted him to be the second in command in Egypt. The king went further and also favored Joseph's entire family when he gave them the best land in Egypt and offered them jobs as his chief herdsmen (Genesis 45:5-6).

- The Israelites acquired wealth from the Egyptians when God set them free. They received silver, gold, and clothing because of God's favor (Exodus 12:35-36).

- King Solomon was looked upon favorably by other rulers because of the wisdom of God upon his life. The other leaders honored him with gifts that added to his wealth (1 Kings 10:1-2, 11-12).

In conclusion, Psalm 5:11-12 summarizes this point well. The passage says that those who put their trust in God and love His name will rejoice. We will shout in joy because the Lord will defend us. He surrounds the righteous with blessings and favor. The favor of God will protect us like a shield.

4. The Gift of Miracles

Through the gift of miracles, God makes things appear or disappear. It is this type of power that God uses to create things out of nothing.

This gift of the Spirit is one of God's channels of provision.

It is through this gift of miracles that Jesus multiplied food for the multitude in John 6:5-12. In another demonstration of this gift of the Spirit, the Lord made money appear in the mouth of the fish (Matthew 17:27).

The Bible records many other instances where God provided for His people through this channel:

• A ram appeared in the thicket when Abraham was about to sacrifice his son Isaac. Because of this experience, Abraham named that place 'Jehovah Jireh' or 'The-Lord-Will-Provide'. (Genesis 22:13-14)

• Manna rained down from heaven, and water flowed from rocks for the Israelites during their forty-year journey in the desert (Exodus 16:4, Nehemiah 9:15).

• Oil miraculously appeared in the vessels that the widow collected in obedience to Elisha's instructions. The widow sold the oil, paid all her debts, and lived on the rest of the money (2 Kings 4:2-7).

• God multiplied the flour and oil of the widow of Zarephath. Through this miracle, Elijah, the widow, and her son had enough for themselves throughout the severe drought and famine, which hit Israel for seven years (1 Kings 17:14-16).

• Two times, the angel brought Elijah food. The food was able to sustain the prophet for forty days as he traveled to the mountain of God (1 Kings 19:5-8).

5. The Gift of the Word of Wisdom

A word of wisdom is a word of instruction. When God tells us to go right or left, to do this or that, He is giving us a word of wisdom.

God will always provide for us when we obey His directions. We can be sure that He has prepared the way ahead of us.

That is what happened when the Lord sent His disciples to go ahead and get a colt for Him to ride on as He entered Jerusalem.

The Bible narrates,

> **11** Now when they drew near to Jerusalem, to Bethphage
> and Bethany, at the Mount of Olives, Jesus sent two of
> his disciples 2 and said to them, "Go into the village in
> front of you, and immediately as you enter it you will
> find a colt tied, on which no one has ever sat. Untie it
> and bring it. 3 If anyone says to you, 'Why are you doing
> this?' say, 'The Lord has need of it and will send it back
> here immediately.'" 4 And they went away and found a
> colt tied at a door outside in the street, and they untied
> it. 5 And some of those standing there said to them,
> "What are you doing, untying the colt?" 6 And they told
> them what Jesus had said, and they let them go. (Mark
> 11:1-6, ESV)

A similar thing happened when He sent two of His disciples to go ahead to prepare for the Passover in Mark 14:12-16 (ESV) :

> 12 And on the first day of Unleavened Bread, when
> they sacrificed the Passover lamb, his disciples said
> to him, "Where will you have us go and prepare for
> you to eat the Passover?" 13 And he sent two of his
> disciples and said to them, "Go into the city, and a man
> carrying a jar of water will meet you. Follow him, 14 and
> wherever he enters, say to the master of the house, 'The
> Teacher says, Where is my guest room, where I may eat
> the Passover with my disciples?' 15 And he will show
> you a large upper room furnished and ready; there
> prepare for us." 16 And the disciples set out and went to
> the city and found it just as he had told them, and they
> prepared the Passover.

Here's a list of other instances of God providing through the manifestation of the gift of the word of wisdom:

• Elijah received precise instructions to go to the Brook Cherith. There, God provided for him most unusually — Ravens brought food daily (1 Kings 17:2-6).

• God told Jacob to go and settle in Egypt after he had learned that Joseph was alive and ruling as the governor of Egypt (Genesis 46:2-4). Later, we learn that the Lord wanted Jacob and his entire family to go to Egypt to save them from the famine that was going to ravage the lands for seven years (Genesis 50:19-21).

• The Lord saved the Shunammite woman and her family from famine. The prophet Elisha instructed her to go to the land of the Philistines for seven years because a great famine was going to hit Israel (2 Kings 8:1-2).

Testifying of God's Provision

God's desire has always been to bring souls to the knowledge of Jesus Christ. And, our testimonies of Jesus' love demonstrated through His provision are a crucial tool in evangelism. Through our witnessing, people will come to Christ. Souls will be saved. Therefore, we should not neglect this tool.

Many times after Jesus had performed a miracle for those who had come to Him, the Lord instructed them to go back and tell others about what He had done (Luke 8:39, Mark 5:19).

The importance of testimonies is not only emphasized in the New Testament, the Old Testament also reiterates it.

An example is when God provided for Israel. He instructed Moses to store a piece of the manna as a testimony for the successive generations (Exodus 16:32).

In addition, Isaiah wrote that he would mention the loving-kindness of the Lord to all people. The prophet wanted everyone to know how much God had loved Israel. He wanted people to understand how good God has been to the nation throughout the generations (Isaiah 63:7).

We should do the same. Let's not belittle the impact that our testimonies have. Let us help the faith of others by telling them about the Father's provision. Let us tell everyone around us about the goodness the Lord has shown us each time He does.

16. Traps of Wealth

Having wealth is a good thing. However, riches come with temptations against which we must guard. God, knowing too well the risks associated with His material blessings, warned Israel in Deuteronomy 8:10-18.

In the passage, Israel was about to step into Canaan where they would have an abundance of everything — silver, gold, herds, flocks, houses, and all types of food. Therefore, God forewarned them not to forget His ways. The Lord reminded Israel that He was the Source of their ability to make wealth. He wanted them to remember how He had taken them out of Egypt, where they were slaves, and then led them through the wilderness.

For their own sake, God had taught Israel to rely on Him when He supernaturally provided water from the rock and fed them with manna. As a result, Israel's humility (reliance on God) had been strengthened. In fact, dependence on the Lord was one of the most important lessons God wanted them to learn during those forty years.

God warned them that they would decline if they forgot from where they and their forefathers had come. Israel would begin to wane to the point of losing everything they owned if they made the mistake of abandoning Him.

Moreover, the Lord gave Moses a song to always remind the nation not to forget that it was Him who had given them all their possessions (Deuteronomy 32:10-15).

The same warning applies to us today. We have to be aware of the following pitfalls that come with riches so that we don't fall away from our relationship with God after He blesses us:

1. Complacency

Being complacent could be defined as the state of not being aware of how bad one's life is. In this state, a person is so engrossed in past victories and blessings that they are not aware of the wrong turn their life has taken.

That was the reality in Israel during Zephaniah's time. The Israelites got so focused on their riches that they forgot about walking in God's ways. It got to a point where some were essentially saying that God does not exist without realizing that it is Him who, over successive generations, had given them the blessings they were enjoying.

Zephaniah 1:12-13 says,

> **12** And it shall come to pass at that time
> *That* I will search Jerusalem with lamps,
> And punish the men
> Who are settled in complacency,
> Who say in their heart,
> 'The Lord will not do good,
> Nor will He do evil.'
> **13** Therefore their goods shall become booty,
> And their houses a desolation;
> They shall build houses, but not inhabit *them;*
> They shall plant vineyards, but not drink their wine.

Notice how some were saying that God would neither do

good nor would He do evil. This means that, according to them, the Lord did not exist.

God wanted Israel to turn back to Him and so He responded. He eventually took Israel's riches away to get them to realize their fallen state.

Reflecting on the present, complacency plagues a lot of wealthy countries, most of which were at the forefront of spreading the Gospel at some point.

Many forget that God, faithful to His word which promises blessings to the descendants of His people to the thousandth generation, has indeed prospered the subsequent generations even if they may not have lived for Him (Deuteronomy 28). As a result, these countries have become very wealthy.

Sadly, the younger generations have lost the knowledge of God. Ironically, people have forgotten the Source, while they enjoy His blessings upon their nations.

2. Pride

> *17* ***Command those who are rich in this present age not to be haughty, nor to trust in uncertain riches but in the living God, who gives us richly all things to enjoy.*** *18 Let them do good, that they be rich in good works, ready to give, willing to share, 19 storing up for themselves a good foundation for the time to come, that they may lay hold on eternal life.*
>
> *– Timothy 6:17-19 (emphasis added)*

Pride can be a pitfall of riches in two aspects: in our relationships with one another and our relationship with God.

Let's start with our relationships with one another:

Financial resources result in influence or some level of authority. That is why Proverbs 22:7 tells us that those who are rich rule over the poor and those who borrow are subject to the lender.

That influence comes because people who are relying on us to support them in one way or another will most likely heed our voice. Others will look up to those who are financially prosperous as role models.

The trap is that we could easily be tempted to elevate ourselves above everybody else because others are depending on us.

As Christians, instead of falling for pride in this way, we should use our influence to do good to others and to promote the kingdom of God.

In terms of our relationship with God, the trap is that a person may not see the need for Jesus because they can meet all their needs. In this mindset, money is the answer to everything. The trust of a man rests on wealth, and consequently, there is no need for faith in the Lord.

This is precisely what the Lord was warning about in the famous and often misinterpreted passage in Matthew 19:21-26:

The Eye of a Needle

In the passage, a wealthy young ruler came to the Lord, asking what he could do to inherit eternal life. Jesus Christ characteristically threw the question back to him. The Lord asked him what the commandments stated. The young man responded by listing them and then noting that he had observed them strictly.

Jesus didn't refute the young ruler's claim that he was a strict observer of the Law. Instead, the Lord told him to sell all his possessions and then follow Him. The rich young man became sad and walked away because he couldn't bring himself to obey by selling everything he owned, giving the proceeds away and then following Jesus Christ.

Following that incident, the Lord said that it is easier for a camel to go through the eye of a needle than for a rich man to enter the kingdom of God.

The church has debated the implications of that statement:

Some argue that Jesus intended to communicate that a wealthy person can't make it to heaven since a camel can't go through the eye of a sewing needle.

Others have claimed that the 'eye of the needle' is not referring to the eye of a sewing needle. It is a metaphor for a narrow gate. The consequence of this argument is that it is difficult, but not impossible, for a rich man to enter the kingdom of God.

My stance on this is that, as in all cases, the Bible explains itself. That very passage, in verses 25-27, reveals what the Lord was talking about.

Matthew 19:25-27 (emphasis added) narrates:

> 25 When His disciples heard *it,* they were greatly astonished, saying, "**Who then can be saved?**"
> 26 But Jesus looked at *them* and said to them, "**With men this is impossible, but with God all things are possible.**"
> 27 Then Peter answered and said to Him, "**See, we have**

left all and followed You. Therefore what shall we have?"

Let's delve into these verses more deeply:

• In verse 25, the disciples were very surprised at Jesus' response and asked who can be saved. The question is why the disciples responded in shock. Clearly, they were wondering who could be saved if the rich young man couldn't make it.

To begin with, we should note these three things:

1) The rich young ruler was a faithful observer of the Law.
2) The Lord told him that there was something he was still missing.
3) Jesus instructed him to sell everything, give the proceeds to the needy, and then follow Him, but the man refused.

Those three facts about the rich young man mean that:

1) He believed that the way to be saved was through a strict and complete observance of the Law.
2) He put his trust in his wealth and so was not willing to give it up to follow Jesus. He essentially rejected the offer to follow Christ because of the money he had accumulated.

Therefore, the reaction of the disciples indicates that at least some of them held the same beliefs as the rich young ruler. Since the disciples had already given up family and properties for the sake of following the Lord, the logical conclusion is that some of them thought that the young ruler had a better chance of making it to heaven because he was a faithful observer of the Law of Moses.

• In verse 26, Jesus explained that **salvation is impossible by man's strength. It is only possible through the grace of**

God.

In other words, Jesus was saying that no one can be saved by strict observance of the Law. Galatians 2:16, 3:11 adds that the Law could not justify anyone because no one could keep it entirely. We can only be saved by the grace of God, which we access through faith in Jesus Christ.

• In verse 27, Peter responded by noting that he, together with the other disciples, had wholly followed Jesus Christ. The apostle then asked what they would gain for putting their faith in the Lord and not on something else.

Therefore, unlike the rich young ruler, Peter and the apostles hadn't allowed their wealth to hinder them from having faith in Jesus and, consequently, following Him.

Summary

Note that Jesus was addressing two issues in this incident:

1) Salvation is by grace through faith in Jesus
and not by the works of the Law.
2) Wealth can be a hindrance to a person's faith in
Jesus. If we reject the offer to follow Jesus for the sake
of anything else, such as wealth, we will not be saved

Furthermore, Peter's response that they had wholly followed the Lord underlines that the issue in discussion was faith in the Lord and the fact that the rich young man's wealth had been a stumbling block to him. He chose to keep his wealth rather than follow Christ.

The Fleeting Power of Money

The word of God is very sobering when it comes to the subject of the power of money. The Scriptures are emphatic that trusting in riches is lacking foresight.

The Bible states that riches can't wipe away our sins, nor those of others, nor enable us to live eternally. Money can't save anyone from death. (Psalm 49:6-9, 16-20)

In reality, the futility of putting our trust in riches becomes evident at the time of death when everything is left behind and the only thing that matters is the relationship we have with God.
Therefore, may we have the wisdom to pray that God will keep us in check by reminding us that we are frail and our days on earth will come to an end. May we always keep in mind that the life of a man is short. May we remember that all the riches we gather will be left behind (Psalm 39:4-6).

God's Correction
There's a principle in the Bible that God corrects His children when pride builds up in them. We see this in Paul's life.

In 2 Corinthians 12:7-10, the apostle testified that a thorn was given to him so that he would not be elevated in pride because of the great grace the Lord had given him. Through this experience, Paul realized that humility made him strong in the Lord because Jesus's strength is made perfect in weakness. As a result, the apostle matured so much that he began to appreciate every experience that reminded him of how, being human, he was weak.

In another example, Hosea testified that God had to humble Israel because of their pride. The prophet warned that the Lord would take away the grain and wine He had given them for food, and the wool and linen He had provided for clothing. The Lord was going to do this so that Israel may learn the He is the Source and not the Baals they were worshipping (Hosea 2:8-9).

Understanding this principle of God's correction calls for self-searching to make sure that we are not falling into complacency or pride. We should be quick to correct ourselves at the slightest hint of the Lord's correction.

When things suddenly stop working out and financial hardship comes where there was abundance, could it be that we have fallen for one of the traps of wealth?

Remember, the Bible warns us that we will not prosper when we stop seeking God. When we forsake Him, He will leave us alone (2 Chronicles 24:19-20). However, without Him, we can do nothing (John 115:5).

17. Generosity

When we study the Scriptures, we find that there's an expectation that the righteous also be generous.

For example, Psalm 112:5, 9 declares,

> [5] A good man deals graciously and lends;
> He will guide his affairs with discretion."
> ...
> [9] He has dispersed abroad,
> He has given to the poor;
> His righteousness endures forever;
> His horn will be exalted with honor.

The life of Job illustrates this notion. For him, being righteous and being generous were inseparable. That is why he defended his righteousness by saying that he had been generous. Job stated that he didn't deserve the calamities that had befallen him because he had given to the poor (Job 31:16-23).

The expectation for the righteous to be generous makes sense because, as believers in Christ, we ought to have the love of God in our hearts (Romans 5:5). Consequently, we can't help but meet the needs we see around us as God's love compels us to act.

It is essential to understand that all of us can afford to be generous. Generosity is not reserved for the wealthy only. Neither is it exclusively for the poor. All of us can be generous because our giving should be according to whatever we have.

Paul's letters to the Corinthians clarify this:

• 2 Corinthians 8:12 (ESV) says, "[12] For if the readiness is there, **it is acceptable according to what a person has, not according to what he does not have**."

• Again, in 1 Corinthians 16:2 (ESV), it is written, "[2] On the first day of every week, **each of you is to put something aside and store it up, as he may prosper**, so that there will be no collecting when I come."

Therefore, we should demonstrate generosity towards our families, friends, and all those that God brings along our path.

We shouldn't neglect the work of the Gospel either. God made it abundantly clear that we should support His work through tithes and offerings.

In Haggai 1:6-11 (ESV), the Lord declared,

> "[6] You have sown much, and harvested little. You eat, but you never have enough; you drink, but you never have your fill. You clothe yourselves, but no one is warm. And he who earns wages does so to put them into a bag with holes."
> [7] Thus says the Lord of hosts: "Consider your ways. [8] Go up to the hills and bring wood and build the house, that I may take pleasure in it and that I may be glorified," says the Lord. [9] "You looked for much, and behold, it came to little. And when you brought it home, I blew it away. Why? declares the Lord of hosts. Because of my

house that lies in ruins, while each of you busies himself with his own house. [10] Therefore the heavens above you have withheld the dew, and the earth has withheld its produce. [11] And I have called for a drought on the land and the hills, on the grain, the new wine, the oil, on what the ground brings forth, on man and beast, and on all their labors."

God's Promises to the Generous:

• God promises to preserve and keep healthy those who are generous (Psalm 41:1-3).

• The Lord will increase the prosperity of those who give (Proverbs 11:24-25, Proverbs 22:9, Proverbs 28:8).

To illustrate, the prophet Daniel understood that God's blessing is upon the generous. That is why he advised King Nebuchadnezzar to repent from his sinful life and then show mercy and kindness to the poor. By doing so, God could have changed the judgment that He had pronounced upon the king and instead lengthened his prosperity (Daniel 4:27).

• The generous will have peace and protection from evil (Psalm 112:5-8).

• The Lord will extend His blessing upon their descendants (Psalm 37:25-26).

• God will visit the generous to bring them salvation and save them from trouble.

There are many stories in the Bible where God performed supernatural acts for people because of their generosity.

An example of this is Abraham and his nephew Lot, who

were both very wealthy and generous (Genesis 13:5-6, 8-9).

Both of them received angelic visitations and supernatural interventions because they were willing to share with strangers:

Abraham was sitting at the door of his tent in the heat of the day when he saw three men approaching and decided to invite them to his tent to have a meal. Those men happened to be the Lord and His angels.

The result of this act of kindness was that Abraham received a promise that Sarah would conceive and give birth to a son within a year (Genesis 18:1-8).

Lot had a very similar experience. He decided to host 'strangers' who had nowhere to sleep – he had found them in the city square.

The 'strangers' turned out to be the angels who had been with the Lord when He talked to Abraham. They ended up saving him and his family from being destroyed (Genesis 19:1-3).

We see this pattern repeated in the book of Acts with Cornelius, who was also wealthy and generous. An angel appeared to him saying that God had remembered his prayers and giving.

In obedience to the angel's instruction, Cornelius sent for Peter, who preached to him, his entire family, and servants. They all received Jesus Christ, the baptism of the Spirit, and baptism in water! (Acts 10:1-6, 44-46)

18. The Conclusion

The book of Ecclesiastes was written by King Solomon, who was the wealthiest person of his time. He devoted the entire book to discussing the meaning of life.

Solomon decided to find the answer to this question by experimenting with his own life. He gratified himself with all kinds of pleasures like wine. He also gathered silver, gold, and unique treasures. The king also did great works like building himself houses and planting great vineyards. He made gardens and orchards and planted all kinds of fruit trees in them. He acquired male and female servants and had more possessions than everyone in Jerusalem (Ecclesiastes 3:1-8).

At the end of his experiment, King Solomon noted,

> [11] Then I looked on all the works that my hands had done
> And on the labor in which I had toiled;
> And indeed all *was* vanity and grasping for the wind.
> *There was* no profit under the sun. (Ecclesiastes 2:11)

What happened was that the king realized that God put eternity in the hearts of men (Ecclesiastes 3:11). That means that nothing will satisfy a person's heart other than that which has eternal value.

Secondly, Solomon added,

> [12] I know that nothing *is* better for them than to rejoice, and to do good in their lives, [13] and also that every man should eat and drink and enjoy the good of all his labor—it *is* the gift of God. (Ecclesiastes 3:12-13).

These two lessons should always be guiding principles for our lives as Christians:

Let us focus on eternity. The Lord taught us to put the kingdom of God and His righteousness first (Matthew 6:33). God will withhold nothing from us when we are committed to Him and are full of love for humanity.

Solomon himself is an example of what God is willing to do when we prioritize His kingdom and are full of love for others. Recall that God was so pleased with the king because his main concern was the people of Israel. Solomon was motivated by love and a desire to see the kingdom of Israel prosper. When God saw that, He added great riches on top of the wisdom the king had requested.

All in all, we should demonstrate the love of Christ by doing good whenever we have an opportunity and also enjoy the blessings that God graciously gives us through Jesus. It is God's will that we do good and enjoy our lives!

Acknowledgments

With sincere gratitude, I wish to appreciate my wife, Zunelly, my family and friends for their tremendous support throughout the process of writing this book. I am so grateful for all the hours spent reading the manuscript and giving their suggestions—this project would not have been possible without their input. Most of all, I give thanks to Jesus for birthing this project in me through a dream, and for His divine inspiration as I was writing this book. May it serve as a blessing to the Body of Christ!

About The Author

Donvan Ochieng' Odhiambo

Donvan has written, co-written and edited multiple Christian faith-based books on a variety of topics such as faith, wealth, generosity, leadership, excellence and humility, among others. Some of his works are forthcoming. He is a graduate of Amherst College and lives with his wife, Zunelly, in Massachusetts.

Books By This Author

The Judgment Seat Of Jesus Christ

Holiness, A Strong Foundation

Building Faith For The Journey

The Path Of Unfailing Love

God's Will, The Excellent Path

Biblical Teachings And Prophecies About The End-Times: Events Until The Rapture

The Path Of Humility

The Path Of Generosity

To Be Sought After: Biblical Keys To Successful Careers

Grace: Enabled By God

Victorious In Life: Experiencing The Life God Intends

Lessons To Enhance Leadership

Friendship: A Biblical Perspective

Made in the USA
Monee, IL
04 November 2026

67380839R00075